Learning to Trust

A Study in Ruth and Esther

By: Caitlyn Burns

Learning to Trust: A Study in Ruth and Esther
Copyright © 2015 by Caitlyn Burns

ISBN 978-0-99-691790-2

Cover Design: Brittany Castellano
Editor: Linda Stubblefield
Interior Design: Caitlyn Burns

Printed in the United States of America

Dedication

To my family, I could not have done any of this without all of their love, support, and encouragement.

I love you all so much!

Table of Contents

Foreword

My dear sister-in-Christ, as I have been writing this study, I have been praying for you. I pray that God would use this study to help you learn more about who He is, how He works, and how much He loves YOU! Don't forget to begin each day in prayer. Ask Him to show you something new as you go through each day's lesson. He is faithful to do exactly that.

I am so excited to be on this journey with you, and to be learning about two amazing women of the Bible: Ruth and Esther. Through their examples, I have learned much about how my life as a woman of God should be. I pray that you will glean as much as you can, and apply each and everything you learn to your own life.

You will read about the choices that our featured women made, as well as others who are in each book. Choices are surely important! I pray that you will take this study to heart, and apply the lessons that you learn in the study to your own personal life.

"Our choices reveal the kind of person we are, but there is another side to the coin. We may, by our choices, also determine what kind of person we will become."

– A. W. Tozer[1]

Caitlyn Burns

Ruth

An Introduction to Ruth

The book of Ruth is one of both suffering and blessing. The storyline follows Naomi and Ruth through both the hard times and the times of God's blessings. Psalm 30:5 correlates perfectly with the theme of the book: *"...weeping may endure for a night, but joy comes in the morning."* This book of Ruth is also considered one of the greatest love stories in the Bible.

Ruth may only be four chapters long, but this powerful book shows how God wants to redeem man exactly like Boaz redeemed Ruth. God wants to be your Kinsman-Redeemer! Please allow Him to do exactly that, and fully surrender everything to Him over these next few weeks. Our Heavenly Father simply wants to know you and to have a personal relationship with you.

Ruth 1 and 2

"Wherever you go, I will go; wherever you live, I will live. Your people will be my people, and your God will be my God."

(Ruth 1:16 NLT)

Day One

Read through the entire book of Ruth before you start on today's lesson. Can you think of a few themes that emerge in the book? One theme I see in particular is obedience, which is not only wanting to do the Father's will, but acting in accordance to His will.

"Therefore let those who suffer according to the will of God commit their souls to Him in doing good, as to a faithful Creator" (1 Peter 4:19).

What a powerful verse! Can't see you see how true this is in Ruth's life?! She suffered much in the beginning of the book, but she was faithful to Him through it all! She was such a testimony to those around her and now to us as well.

1. By reading key details in Ruth, chapters 1 through 4, we can ascertain an idea of how many years the book of Ruth spans. Read the following verses, and draw a timeline underneath the verses.

   Ruth 1:4, Ruth 1:22, and Ruth 2:3 (mid-April to mid-June), Ruth 3:1-18, Ruth 4:1-22

2. In the margin, write down any truth that stands out to you, any questions, or thoughts that you have on the following passage.

"Now it came to pass, in the days when the judges ruled, that there was a famine in the land. And a certain man of Bethlehem, Judah, went to dwell in the country of Moab, he and his wife and his two sons.

[2]The name of the man was Elimelech, the name of his wife was Naomi, and the names of his two sons were Mahlon and Chilion—Ephrathites of Bethlehem, Judah. And they went to the country of Moab and remained there.

[3]Then Elimelech, Naomi's husband, died; and she was left, and her two sons.

[4]Now they took wives of the women of Moab: the name of the one was Orpah, and the name of the other Ruth. And they dwelt there about ten years.

[5]Then both Mahlon and Chilion also died; so the woman survived her two sons and her husband.

[6]Then she arose with her daughters-in-law that she might return from the country of Moab, for she had heard in the country of Moab that the Lord had visited His people by giving them bread.

[7]Therefore she went out from the place where she was, and her two daughters-in-law with her; and they went on the way to return to the land of Judah.

[8]And Naomi said to her two daughters-in-law, "Go, return each to her mother's house. The Lord deal kindly with you, as you have dealt with the dead and with me.

[9]The Lord grant that you may find rest, each in the house of her husband." So she kissed them, and they lifted up their voices and wept.

[10]And they said to her, "Surely we will return with you to your people" (Ruth 1:1-10).

3. Where does the book of Ruth take place?

Ruth lived when the judges ruled Israel—a period of time when lawlessness and faithlessness reigned. The judges ruled from approximately 1400 to 1050 B.C. Judges 21:25 describes the time frame quite well: *"In those days there was no king in Israel; everyone did what was right in his own eyes."*

What a dangerous time in which to live! Living in an age when people did what was described as "right" in their own eyes, without any moral standard seems outrageous, but that portrayal is how God described this time.

4. Using the following verses, write down a few words that describe the meaning of each verse. For example, Deuteronomy 12:8 (*"Everyone did what was right in his own eyes…"*)

Judges 17:6

Judges 21:25

Proverbs 12:15

Proverbs 21:2

The Hebrew word for the city of Bethlehem is *Beth Lehem* which means "house of bread." Bethlehem is located about six miles south of Jerusalem.

Famine. Famine. Famine. Ruth 1:1 and 2 reveal that one of the main reasons why Elimelech and Naomi relocated from Bethlehem to Moab was because of the famine in the land. In Leviticus 26:3, 4, God tells why He would allow a famine in the Promised Land: *"If you walk in My statutes and keep My commandments, and perform them, ⁴then I will give you rain in its season, the land shall yield its produce, and the trees of the field shall yield their fruit."*

The Israelite nation had not been walking in God's statutes nor keeping His commandments. The famine came because of their disobedience to Him. Famine comes when rain ceases. Only the Lord can bring rain, which causes the crops to grow and produce food.

While I can understand why Elimelech took his family to another country in order to provide for his family; however, I cannot understand his choice of places. Moab is a city in a heathen nation—a land that was far from God and full of pagan gods.

5. Read Psalm 108:9. After you have read the verse, write it down word-for-word in the space provided.

6. Why do you think God thinks of Moab as a washpot?

7. The following verses will help explain exactly why the Lord feels this way about Moab. Write a summary of a few words underneath each verse.

   Jeremiah 48:7

Jeremiah 48:29

Jeremiah 48:42

8. To understand the origins of the Moabite nation, read Genesis 19:30-38 and write a brief explanation of how the Moabite tribe began:

Moab originated when Lot and his oldest daughter had a child together. Lot's daughter named the child Moab, who later became the father of the Moabite nation. Throughout the Bible, the Jews and the Moabites clashed in many different encounters.

a) Balak, the king of Moab, opposed the Jewish prophet Balaam (Numbers 22-25)
b) Moab oppressed Israel for eighteen years (Judges 3:12-30)
c) Saul crushed the Moabites (1 Samuel 14:47).
d) Moab fought against Israel (2 Kings 3:5-27).

9. God cursed the nation of Moab because of their worship of the god Chemosh and their continual opposition toward God's chosen people. Dig deeper into why God cursed this nation. Doing some background research will reveal the names of the gods of the Moabites.

1 Kings 11:7

2 Kings 3:26-26

The god, Chemosh, the chief of the Moabite deities, required child sacrifice. Can you imagine sacrificing your child to a god?! I can't even begin to imagine what making that sacrifice would be like! Envision serving a god who not only does not hear you nor has a relationship with you, but one to whom you must sacrifice your child to in order to please him. I am so thankful that I serve a God Who loves me unconditionally, has my best interest in mind, wants to have a relationship with me, and Who sent His only Son to die on the cross for my sins. He is the God I want to serve for the rest of my life!

Take a few moments and thank God for all that He has done for you and will do for you! Remember what an amazing God we serve!

10. Read Luke 15:11-32. In your own words, describe how Elimelech's family is similar to the prodigal son.

11. Write down this week's memory verse, Ruth 1:16, in the space provided. Writing it down will help you to remember the words. If you need to say it out loud a few times, do it!

Day Two

Ruth is one of my favorite women in the Bible to emulate. Her example is astounding! Today we will be learning from the life of Naomi as well as the life of Ruth, and how God was faithful to lead them each step of the way. His plans for their lives were better than they could have thought, but they had to go through trials before they saw the blessings God had for them.

You may be going through a trial right now, and you do not understand why God is taking you through this situation. Simply trust that God is working in your life. He is faithful!

Ask the Lord to show you His faithfulness in your life just as He did in the lives of both Ruth and Naomi.

1. I love to dig deep into the names in the Bible and find the meaning. Names in the Bible are important because they help us understand more about the person. Some people in the Bible are unnamed, such as the woman at the well and Lot's wife. I believe that God placing a name in the Bible is of great importance. The sons of Naomi and Elimelech, Mahlon and Chilion, are a testament to that fact. The name *Mahlon* means "weakling," and *Chilion* means "sickly." Poor boys. Their names did not give them much to live up to. Beyond Ruth 1:1-5, nothing more is mentioned about these two men. Their death was recorded in verse 5.

   Naomi means "pleasant," *Elimelech* means "my God is king," *Orpah* means "the stiff-necked one," and *Ruth* means "faithful friend." Of all of these names, Ruth is my favorite. After all, who wouldn't want a name that means "faithful friend"?

   When looking into the meaning of names, I also researched my name, and I discovered the meaning of *Caitlyn* is "pure one" or "innocent." I want to live up to my name—to be a "pure one" and "innocent" in the sight of God.

Look up your name and use the space below to record the etymology and history of your name.

2. Imagine yourself in Naomi's shoes. You have moved away from the town you loved, leaving behind everything you knew, and losing both your husband and your two sons. Naomi somewhat reminds me of Job. Everything Job loved was taken away from him, yet Job never felt that God had abandoned him. He was walking through "the valley of the shadow of death" that David mentions in Psalm 23. Naomi is journeying the same path. Her faith is being tested. Frances Vander Velde says it perfectly, "God was loving Naomi all the while that He was leading her through the shadows." [2] God loved Naomi more than she could ever humanly understand. He had a far better plan for her life—one of blessing.

Every child of God faces the same challenges that Naomi faced with trusting God with her future. The Lord has given me three verses that have encouraged me through the difficult times when I don't understand what God is doing. Look up the verses below and write down how they can encourage you.

Romans 8:28

Jeremiah 29:11

Isaiah 55:8, 9

When Naomi hears news in Moab that the Lord is providing food for the people in Bethlehem, the longing to be in Bethlehem surfaces. She hears of how the Lord is blessing her hometown. The Bible says that Elimelech had originally moved his family to Moab because of the famine in Bethlehem-Judah. Sadly, he did not trust God to provide for his everyday needs. He did not trust God to take care of his family with the complete faith that God would do as He had promised. God is the only One Who could end the famine, and He did.

Time and time again, both the Old Testament and the New Testament reveal how God miraculously provides for His children. He provided manna for the Israelites in the desert. He provided water for the children of Israel in Rephidim in Exodus 17. God cares so very much about all of His children's needs!

Philippians 4:19, *"And my God shall supply all your need according to His riches in glory by Christ Jesus."* This verse in Philippians has given me hope that He cares for my needs even when I don't sense Him being there. All I need to do is ask Him in faithfulness because He wants to give His children every good thing.

3. In the days of the book of Ruth, the Jews were forbidden to marry women who were Gentiles. God had specific instructions as to why the Jews were not allowed to marry the Gentiles. After reading each verse, write down why God instructed the Israelites to not marry those who worshipped idols.

   Deuteronomy 7:3-7

   Deuteronomy 23:3-7

   Nehemiah 13:1-3

4. Why do you think Naomi and Elimelech allowed their sons to marry Moabite women after God had specifically instructed the Jews not to marry Gentiles?

5. My favorite passage in the book of Ruth is found in Ruth 1:16, 17. *"But Ruth replied, 'Don't urge me to leave you or to turn back from you. Where you go I will go, and where you stay I will stay. Your people will be my people and your God my God. ¹⁷Where you die I will die, and there I will be buried. May the LORD deal with me, be it ever so severely, if even death separates you and me'"* (NIV). Oh, the wonderful promise Ruth made to her mother-in-law! Ruth was willingly giving up everything she had known and loved—her family, her culture, and her home. She was ready to give it all up to follow the Lord. Our heroine left all she had to follow a God in Whom she was beginning to trust. Can you say that, like Ruth, you would be willing to give up everything to follow God?

Read Matthew 10:37-39 and Luke 18:29-30. What does Christ promise those who leave behind everything and follow Him?

Ruth is learning that following God is always an adventure—one that is well worth the cost in the end.

When I was eleven years old, the Lord directed my parents to take a six-month ministry opportunity in the country of India. My mom and I had visited there a couple times but only for two weeks at a time. Six months, however, meant leaving everything behind and adapting to an entirely different culture and way of living. Our experience has given me a little more of an understanding as to how Ruth could have felt when she left behind the life she had known and had embraced and, instead, trusted God to watch over her.

My favorite story of how God provided for us was in the area of my dad's job. Since we would be leaving the States for six months, my dad needed to quit his job. This decision meant having no income while we were living in India, and no job to provide for our family when we returned home to the States. The day came when my dad told his boss. His boss listened and, to our amazement, gave my dad a six-month leave of absence. Not only would he keep his job, but he would be paid for three of the six months we would be gone. Our God is amazing!! I have seen how He blesses His children above and beyond!!

6. Would you be willing to live in a country where you did not know anybody with the exception of one person? What do you think God could teach you in that circumstance?

7. 2 Corinthians 7:10 describes Ruth's conversion to Christianity. Fill in the blanks for the verse. *"For godly sorrow produces _____ leading to _____ not to be regretted, but the _____ of the _____ produces death."*

Day Three

I know that the more I study and learn from the life of Ruth, the more I want to become like her. Her character, her personal walk with God, and her loyalty are only three of her amazing qualities that I desire for myself. As you begin today's study, ask God to place a desire in your heart to want to become the woman of God that He desires you to be!

1. Ruth placed her entire life in God's hands. She trusted Him with everything that she had and was willing to do anything for Him. In your own life, does trusting God come naturally to you, or is trust something with which you struggle? Why or why not?

"You shall walk after the Lord your God and fear Him, and keep His commandments and obey His voice; you shall serve Him and hold fast to Him" (Deuteronomy 13:4).

"But Naomi said, "Turn back, my daughters; why will you go with me? Are there still sons in my womb, that they may be your husbands? ¹²Turn back, my daughters, go—for I am too old to have a husband. If I should say I have hope, if I should have a husband tonight and should also bear sons, ¹³would you wait for them till they were grown? Would you restrain yourselves from having husbands? No, my daughters; for it grieves me very much for your sakes that the hand of the Lord has gone out against me!" (Ruth 1:11-13).

If you look carefully at these verses, you will see Naomi's pleading for Ruth and Orpah to stay in the land of Moab. As was the custom in Israel, when a wife's husband died, his brother or a near kinsman would take his place and thus carry on the family name. Naomi mentions the custom in verse 11 saying, *"...Are there still sons in my womb, that they may be your husbands?"* Naomi knew she could not provide Ruth and Orpah with another husband to carry on the family name. Naomi had their best interest in mind. God, however, had bigger plans for Ruth.

2. Luke 9:23, 24 tell us what *following Christ* means. Ruth's following Christ meant giving up everything that she knew, and going wherever Christ called her to go. How does this verse apply to every Christian?

3. God promises to take care of His children at all times. Trusting Him to do that, however, does not always come easily. Write out each of the following verses to see how we can trust Him completely.

   Proverbs 3:5, 6

   Isaiah 26:3, 4

   Psalm 37:5

   Deuteronomy 31:8

4. Do you think Ruth made a wise decision to follow Naomi on her return journey to Bethlehem?

5. Consider Ruth's words in verses 16 and 17. Could you display the same unconditional love, courage, and faith?

6. Use the space provided to ask God to give you a love that is similar to the love that Ruth and Naomi shared.

7. Write about a time in your life when you made a decision to follow Christ.

8. Read Matthew 2. In what city is Christ born? To what city did Naomi and Ruth travel back to live in?

How awe-inspiring to see that Ruth lived in the same city in which our Saviour was born! We also know from Ruth chapter 4 that Christ came through the lineage of David, Ruth's great-grandson. How awesome and amazing to know that because of Ruth's faithfulness to the Lord, she was blessed to have Christ come through her lineage.

Treacherous, difficult, and *long* are three words to describe the trip from Moab to Bethlehem. The seventy-mile journey would have been a seven- to ten-day trip. Ruth and Naomi would have descended about 4,500 feet from Moab to the Jordan River valley and then journeyed upward 3,700 feet through the hills of Judah to reach Naomi's hometown.

9. After reading Luke 15:11-20, explain how the story of Naomi is similar to the prodigal son.

"Ah! You will never win any soul to the right by a compromise with the wrong. It is the decision for Christ and his truth that has the greatest power in the family, and the greatest power in the world too." – Charles Spurgeon[3]

As Naomi entered Bethlehem, she quickly set everyone straight by saying, "Call me *Mara*," which means "bitter." Author Larry Crabb writes of Naomi, *"She stood before her community, admitting who she was rather than pretending to be who she should have been."*[4] Naomi is bitter about the circumstances in her life, including her husband's death. Elizabeth George could not have said it any better: "His intent is never to make us bitter—only to make us better."[5]

In doing a little research about bitterness, a place mentioned in the Old Testament named Marah is located in the desert of Shur. Exodus 15:23 and 24 share the reason why this city in the desert was named Marah. In the space provided, write the reason.

Naomi's attitude about being bitter and how her she could not see God's plan ahead of her reminds me of the account of Joseph in Genesis. While Joseph did not have bitterness toward God, he had plenty of opportunities to display that propensity, considering the fact he was sold into slavery by his brothers, was wrongly accused of having an illicit relationship with Potiphar's wife, and was imprisoned for two years—to name a few of the injustices he endured. Joseph did not know how God was working in his life, but Joseph still trusted his Heavenly Father.

One lesson I can always learn from Joseph is to trust that God is working all things for my good. Had Joseph not been sold into slavery, had he not been thrown into prison, had God not given him the answer to the dreams of the baker, the butler and Pharaoh, then Joseph would not have risen to second in command over Egypt and saved his country. Isn't it amazing how God really did work all this for Joseph's good and for the good of those around him?!

Day Four

Today's lesson will address a few topics, such as character, obedience, and God's provision for His children. All of these aspects are important in a believer's life. Ask the Lord to give you great character, obedience in the areas to which He is directing you, and the knowledge that He wants to bless and provide for His children.

1. How does Ruth 2:1-4 describe Boaz's character?

Not only was Boaz a man of great wealth, but a man of character and of valor. As Judges 6:12 says, *"And the Angel of the Lord appeared to him, and said to him, "The LORD is with you, you mighty man of valor!"* Character in a relationship is most important! Boaz also had a reputation that was well-known.

2. How does a person develop a good reputation? Why is having a good reputation important?

3. List some character qualities that you would like in your future spouse.

There is no such thing as a coincidence in the Bible. God does everything for a reason. Ruth didn't simply "happen to come to the part of the field belonging to Boaz." God directed her to Boaz. What a wonderful story that God is beginning to unfold right before Ruth's eyes! *"A man's heart plans his way, But the LORD directs his steps"* (Proverbs 16:9).

4. The Lord had laws set in place that would help care for the poor and the foreigners. Widows, orphans, travelers, the fatherless, and the lame are a few of the categories that would fall under the category of poor and foreign.

   Read Leviticus 19:9, 10 and Leviticus 23:22. Write down what the people were instructed to do concerning the needy and the strangers.

Boaz went above and beyond what the Mosaic law required him to display to widows. He allowed Ruth to glean, and he even instructed the reapers to let additional grain fall on purpose and to allow Ruth to pick them up. As Boaz watched over her, he ordered the reapers not to touch her. Boaz was providing for Ruth and Naomi in ways that they could not even begin to imagine!

5. God always will provide for His children! When has God provided for you?

6. Write down a few ways that Boaz protected Ruth according to Ruth 2:8, 9.

"25 Therefore I say to you, do not worry about your life, what you will eat or what you will drink; nor about your body, what you will put on. Is not life more than food and the body more than clothing?

26 Look at the birds of the air, for they neither sow nor reap nor gather into barns; yet your heavenly Father feeds them. Are you not of more value than they?

27 Which of you by worrying can add one cubit to his stature?

28 So why do you worry about clothing? Consider the lilies of the field, how they grow: they neither toil nor spin;

29 and yet I say to you that even Solomon in all his glory was not arrayed like one of these.

30 Now if God so clothes the grass of the field, which today is, and tomorrow is thrown into the oven, will He not much more clothe you, O you of little faith?

31 Therefore do not worry, saying, 'What shall we eat?' or 'What shall we drink?' or 'What shall we wear?'

32 For after all these things the Gentiles seek. For your heavenly Father knows that you need all these things.

33 But seek first the kingdom of God and His righteousness, and all these things shall be added to you.

34 Therefore do not worry about tomorrow, for tomorrow will worry about its own things. Sufficient for the day is its own trouble" (Matthew 6:25-34).

7. God meant to prosper Ruth's life with what may have seemed like a tragedy in her losing a husband. If you were to zoom in extremely close on a flower, you would see only the middle part, but it would appear to be fuzzy. You would find it quite difficult to tell what the full picture of the flower would be like. The same is true with God. We only see what is in front of us. As much as we want to see the big picture, only God can see it. Of one fact we can be sure: everything He does is for our good—to give us a future and a hope.

Think about a recent trial that God has brought you through. What are a few positives you have seen as a result of the trial?

8. How was God revealed to you during that time of trial?

"Many are the afflictions of the righteous, But the LORD delivers him out of them all" (Psalm 34:19). How true this verse proved to be in the life of Ruth and Naomi! They faced many difficulties in their lives, but the end of the book reveals they came out victorious. God uses trials in our life to perfect us. If we never had any trials in our life, then why would we need help from God?! When we do encounter trials, we can rely on God's Word for encouragement, and take comfort that He is our Deliverer.

9. Read Jeremiah 29:11. Describe the words of hope that God has for you in your walk with Him.

"For whatever things were written before were written for our learning, that we through the patience and comfort of the Scriptures might have hope" (Romans 15:4).

Day Five

Don't forget to pray before you start today's lesson! Ask God to give you a heart after His own. Spend a few minutes as well simply listening to Him. Prayer is our way of talking to Him. I like to think of praying as friendship with God because many times praying can turn into a one-way conversation, but I need to remind myself that I need to take time and listen to what God has to say to me. I encourage you to seek to have a two-way prayer time today!

1. Ruth was a beautiful person—inside and out. Boaz noticed this beauty right away. Godly character radiates, and people notice something different about the person who possesses Godly character. It didn't take Boaz long to notice Ruth! In today's vernacular, you could say he "fell" for Ruth, but he wanted her because of her character. What do your friends say about your character?

2. As you read this chapter, what did you learn about Ruth's character? Make sure to write down what Ruth says or does that explains each quality.

3. God will always bless you for what you do for the poor. Boaz certainly did not have to go the extra mile for Ruth, but he chose to do so. Write down Matthew 19:29, 30.

4. How did Boaz demonstrate Galatians 6:10 to Ruth?

"Therefore, as we have opportunity, let us do good to all, especially to those who are of the household of faith" (Galatians 6:10).

The book of Ruth never records an instance of Ruth's wondering and asking God "Why?" Ruth shows us an attitude of trusting God in every circumstance. Instead of asking God "why" when you don't understand what He is doing in your time of trial, instead ask Him: "How do You want me to be an example to others during this time?" or "How can I comfort others as I am experiencing this time of turmoil?"

5. Read 2 Corinthians 1:3-7 and then fill in the blanks with the missing words:

"_____ be the God and Father of our Lord Jesus Christ, the Father of mercies and God of all _____, ⁴who comforts us in all our tribulation, that we may be able to _____ those who are in any trouble, with the comfort with which we ourselves are comforted by God. ⁵For as the sufferings of _____ abound in us, so our consolation also abounds through Christ. ⁶Now if we are afflicted, it is for your _____ and salvation, which is effective for _____ the same sufferings which we also suffer. Or if we are comforted, it is for your consolation and salvation. ⁷And our hope for you is _____, because we know that as you are partakers of the sufferings, so also you will _____ of the _____."

6. Boaz took Ruth under his wing in many ways. Similar to Boaz, God takes us under His wing: He protects us and loves us; we find our security in Him. Carefully read each of the following verses, and paraphrase what the verse is saying.

Psalm 36:7

Psalm 17:8

Psalm 63:7

Ruth 2:23, *"So she stayed close by the young women of Boaz, to glean until the end of barley harvest and wheat harvest; and she dwelt with her mother-in-law."*

The harvest of barley normally began around mid-April, and the harvest of wheat finished around mid-June. These couple of months required intense labor. The harvest normally coincided with the seven weeks of Passover and the Feast of Weeks, otherwise known as Pentecost.

> *"And you shall count for yourselves from the day after the Sabbath, from the day that you brought the sheaf of the wave offering: seven Sabbaths shall be completed. [16]Count fifty days to the day after the seventh Sabbath; then you shall offer a new grain offering to the LORD. [17]You shall bring from your dwellings two wave loaves of two-tenths of an ephah. They shall be of fine flour; they shall be baked with leaven. They are the firstfruits to the LORD"* (Leviticus 23:15-17).

7. How can you apply what you have learned today to life this week?

8. Write down Ruth 1:16 from memory in the space provided.

"We can't control the circumstances of life, but we can control how we respond to them. That's what faith is all about, daring to believe that God is working everything for our good even when we don't feel like it or see it happening." – Warren Wiersbe[6]

Ruth 3 and 4

*"Charm is deceptive, and beauty does not last; but a woman who fears the L*ORD *will be greatly praised. Reward her for all she has done. Let her deeds publicly declare her praise."*

(Proverbs 31:30, 31 NLT)

Day One

Can you believe you are already halfway through the book of Ruth?! Isn't it amazing?! Ruth has much to teach us, and we have much to learn from both her and Naomi. Ask the Lord to show you exactly what He wants you to learn today.

1. Read Ruth 3 and write down a one sentence summary for the chapter.

2. Write down the instructions that Naomi instructed Ruth to follow in Ruth 3:3.

"…In fact, he is winnowing barley tonight at the threshing floor" (Ruth 3:2). The process of *winnowing* involves tossing the grain in the air, which separates the grain from the chaff. Due to the sifting and bagging of the grain, winnowing normally took place when the Mediterranean winds blew in the late afternoon and continued on until late night. Most likely, Boaz would have stayed throughout the night to watch over the harvested grain to prevent it from being stolen.

The threshing floor was a large, hard-packed area of either earth or stone on the east side of the city. The separating of the grain and the chaff took place on the threshing floor.

3. Once Ruth arrived at the threshing floor, what was she supposed to do?

In today's setting, Ruth's lying down at Boaz's feet may seem to have a connotation of intimacy. However, in that culture at that time, the practice was considered to be an act of total submission. In Bible days, a servant would lie down at the master's feet, ready to answer the master's every command. Naomi knew this custom; thus, she instructed Ruth to offer the gesture of a humble spirit and submission.

> *"Even to the present day, when a Jew marries a woman, he throws the skirt or end of his talith over her to signify that he has taken her under his protection."*
> – Adam Clarke[7]

> *"The spreading of a skirt over a widow as a way of claiming her as a wife is attested among Arabs of early days, and the Joüon [A grammar of Biblical Hebrew] says it still exists among some modern Arabs."* – Leon Morris[8]

4. Ezekiel 16:8 describes a similar action to the one that Ruth asked Boaz to perform; i.e., his taking Ruth under his wing. Write down the verse exactly as your Bible says.

5. How does the Lord spread His covering over us and take care of us?

6. What does 1 Timothy 5:3-16 tell us about widows? Write down the specific instructions that Paul wrote to the younger widows in verse 14.

Paul's expressed God's desire for every young woman to marry, have children, and manage her household. Naomi had the very same agenda for Ruth, and expressed that desire to Ruth from the beginning of the book. I can only think about how God heard Naomi's prayer over Ruth and wished to see the joy in both of their hearts of knowing and seeing God answer their prayers right before them. The end of the book of Ruth unveils the entire fulfillment of Paul's instructions for young widows: Ruth married Boaz, gave birth to Obed, and managed her household.

7. Boaz's statement to Ruth in verse 10 provides a hint that Boaz was quite a bit older than Ruth. What phrase reveals this clue?

8. Why do you think Boaz asked Ruth to leave early in the morning so no one would see her?

9. In the space provided, write this week's memory verse two times.

Day Two

Boaz

Once Boaz entered the picture in the book of Ruth, a level of character can be seen in him that only God can establish in a man. We can do nothing without God's help. The fruit of the Spirit is meaningless without God's help also. Ask the Lord today to instill in you a character that will continue to develop as you grow in your Christian walk. Ask Him to help you with building the fruit of the Spirit in your life as well.

1. Boaz is a remarkable example of a man of character. Using Titus 2:2 and Titus 2:6-8 as your example, write down the character qualities that Boaz displays.

2. Who did Boaz approach in order to take Ruth's hand in marriage?

The gate where Boaz talked with the nearer kinsman-redeemer is where normal business transactions took place.

> *"Now Absalom would rise early and stand beside the way to the gate. So it was, whenever anyone who had a lawsuit came to the king for a decision, that Absalom would call to him and say, "What city are you from?" And he would say, "Your servant is from such and such a tribe of Israel"* (2 Samuel 15:2).

> *"When I went out to the gate by the city, When I took my seat in the open square"* (Job 29:7).

3. List the one reason why the nearer kinsman-redeemer did not want to redeem Ruth? Does this motive seem selfish? Explain your answer.

4. Explain the method used to show that property had been transferred from one person to another?

5. This method, which may seem like a strange way to pass on property, followed the instructions of the Law of Moses in Deuteronomy 25:7-10. Under what circumstance would the kinsman-redeemer remove his shoe?

This tradition is addressed in additional references in the Bible: Deuteronomy 25:5-10, Amos 2:6, and Amos 8:6. The purpose of removing the sandal was a way to "seal the deal," as with the redeeming of Ruth.

6. The law of redemption was a God-given law to protect widows. The following verses will provide a better understanding of what the law entails. Write down what you learn beneath each passage.

Deuteronomy 25:5, 6

Leviticus 25:23-28

7. Another law that God set in place for the Israelites had to do with the land that God gave to them. God's children could not permanently sell the land; however, they could lease that land, which would then be returned to them in the year of the Jubilee. Similar to how Boaz redeemed Ruth, a kinsman-redeemer could redeem the land.

Read Leviticus 25:23-28 and write down the specific instructions that redeeming the land required.

Day Three

"Therefore know that the Lord your God, He is God, the faithful God who keeps covenant and mercy for a thousand generations with those who love Him and keep His commandments" (Deuteronomy 7:9).

What a great verse to start off the day's study! Ruth's story is a perfect reminder of God's faithfulness in the Christian's life. God kept His covenant toward Ruth, and He loved her with a steadfast love. He truly did want the best for Ruth! Say a prayer to God before you begin today's lesson and thank Him for being faithful—even we when are faithless.

1. Who did Boaz approach in order to ask for Ruth's hand in marriage?

2. Boaz is an Old Testament picture of our Kinsman-redeemer, Jesus Christ. After reading I Peter 1:19, write down the Scripture word for word. Writing the verse down as it is exactly in the Bible makes it easier to hide God's Word in our hearts and not simply record our own interpretation on the verse.

   1 Peter 1:19

3. List any similarities between Jesus and Boaz as Kinsman-redeemers.

I can only imagine what it would have been like to be in Ruth's position and see firsthand how the Lord works in our life. Ruth's and Boaz's wedding must have been a wonderful promise of what the future would hold: many blessings. Since we know that Ruth and Boaz are a picture of the relationship between Christ and the church, then ponder for a minute what you think our wedding day with the Lamb will be. Were *wonderful, majestic,* and *powerful* a few of the words that came to mind? Scripture tells us in Revelation 19:7 that we will be glad and give Him all of the riches and honor that are due to His name. On that day, glory will belong to Him for all that He has done for you and me. Such a marvelous day to look forward to—a day when we will meet our Bridegroom face to face!

4. We have learned in the book of Ruth that Boaz is a type of Christ. As Boaz redeemed Ruth, Christ has also redeemed you and me. Read Romans 6 and write down how we are redeemed in Christ.

5. How does Boaz's redeeming of Ruth convey a picture of how Christ redeemed the sinners in Romans 6?

6. Titus 2:3-5 lists exactly what we should be looking for in a mentor, as well as who we are called to be one day for the next generation. Write down the requirements that Paul instructed us to follow.

7. An excellent example to Ruth, Naomi was a woman who lived the principles taught in Titus 2:3-5. What can you learn from Naomi?

8. Think of an older woman who is an example in your own life. What is her name? List a few things you have learned from this lady.

Using Titus 2:3-5 as your guide, fill in the requirements for the older and the younger women.

Older Women

Younger Women

Much can be learned from those women who are older and wiser than we are. Because they have learned from the Lord, we can follow their example of a Godly wife, a role model, a friend, a homemaker, and more! Unfortunately, we rarely see the older women instructing the younger women in the church. We need to change that! God especially placed those three verses in the Bible so we could benefit from them. I highly encourage you to find an older woman who can mentor you. A mentor can be an elderly lady from church, a grandmother whose walk you wish to emulate, your mother, or even a relative.

My mom has been my principal example of a Godly wife, mother, and homemaker. I have been able to glean from her wisdom for what lies ahead in my future—marriage, a family, and a home.

Day Four

I believe it is so important to begin each day in prayer before beginning the day's lesson. Each day ask God to give you the mind, ears, and heart to learn all that He desires for you! You are so precious and special to Him! Keep pressing in to Him. Keep reading His Word. Keep following His path. The book of Ruth has been showing us that He loves us and cares about us more than we can possibly know!

What a blessing Obed's birth must have been to Ruth and Boaz! In Hebrew the name *Obed* means "servant" or "worshipper." God, in His wisdom, set up a way that the family name would be carried on even though Ruth remarried. Deuteronomy 25:6 says, *"And it shall be that the firstborn son which she bears will succeed to the name of his dead brother, that his name may not be blotted out of Israel."* In that way the family name of Ruth's first husband, Mahlon, would be carried on through the firstborn son. Ruth's firstborn was Obed. After the firstborn son carried on the family name, then any further children born would carry on Boaz's name.

1. Who is Obed's son? His grandson?

2. Follow the genealogy lineage in Matthew 1:5-16. Who comes directly from Obed's line?

3. God established a covenant with David in 2 Samuel 1:1-17. What does Ruth's giving birth to Obed have to do with the covenant God established with David?

4. Ruth and Boaz served the Lord through obedience; the blessings they experienced were beyond what they could have dreamed. God will always use our obedience to Him for good! Read the following verses and record them in the space provided.

Deuteronomy 6:18

Proverbs 3:5, 6

2 John 1:6

Deuteronomy 28:2

5. Boaz lived during the period described as the time of the Judges or a time when *"...everyone did what was right in his own eyes"* (Judges 21:25). Knowing this, why do you think Boaz wanted to carefully follow all of the laws that God had established?

6. Think about the sacrifices that Ruth continually made throughout her life. Think about the many blessings she received because of her faith in God. What are some life examples Ruth set that we can learn from and follow?

7. In your own words, summarize the important events that transpired in the book of Ruth.

8. What lessons can be gleaned from the book of Ruth?

Day Five

Ruth truly is a wonderful example of a Proverbs 31 woman! She displays her godly character to all those around her. I know that the thought of being a Proverbs 31 woman today can seem both impossible and even overwhelming. Simply try to figure out how she had time for all of the pursuits listed that she accomplished. The chapter is, in fact, a goal that can be achieved over time; you don't have to do it all in one day. When we first started our journey with Ruth until now, we have seen her transform into a radiant woman of God. Ask the Lord today to help you become an example to the women around you in how you live your life, in your relationship with the Lord, in your singleness or in marriage, in your friendships, or in your ministry.

"Charm is deceitful and beauty is passing, But a woman who fears the Lord, she shall be praised" (Proverbs 31:30).

1. Throughout the book of Ruth, Ruth and Boaz constantly put the Lord and others ahead of themselves. At the time, neither one of them knew how God would bless them. Because we have the Bible, we can see the entire picture; however, this couple did not get to see the whole effect of their choices. The Lord blessed Ruth and Boaz for choosing His will over their own. Write a prayer in the space provided, asking God to help you choose His will for your life.

2. God used every specific detail in the Bible for our learning. Not one word can be considered as "wasted space." Knowing this fact, what did you learn from all of our different characters, and the Lord Whom they served?

Isn't it interesting that Jesus would come through Boaz's lineage? How incredible that God used the son of a prostitute (Rahab) and that through Boaz's marriage to Ruth, the Son of God would come, be born, and dwell in the exact same city!

3. Write down Proverbs 31:30, 31 from memory.

4. Using the verses as your guideline, fill in the table with the qualifications for the Redeemer.

The Qualifications for a Blood Redeemer	Scripture Passages
	Leviticus 25:23-25 Leviticus 25:48, 49 Deuteronomy 25:5, 7-10
	Leviticus 25:25, 26
	Deuteronomy 25:7, 9

5. Use the following verses to fill in the family tree from both Naomi's and Boaz's side of the family.

    Ruth 4:13-22

    Ruth 1:1-5

    1 Samuel 16:6-9

    1 Chronicles 2:14, 15

    1 Chronicles 27:18

Boaz's Family Tree

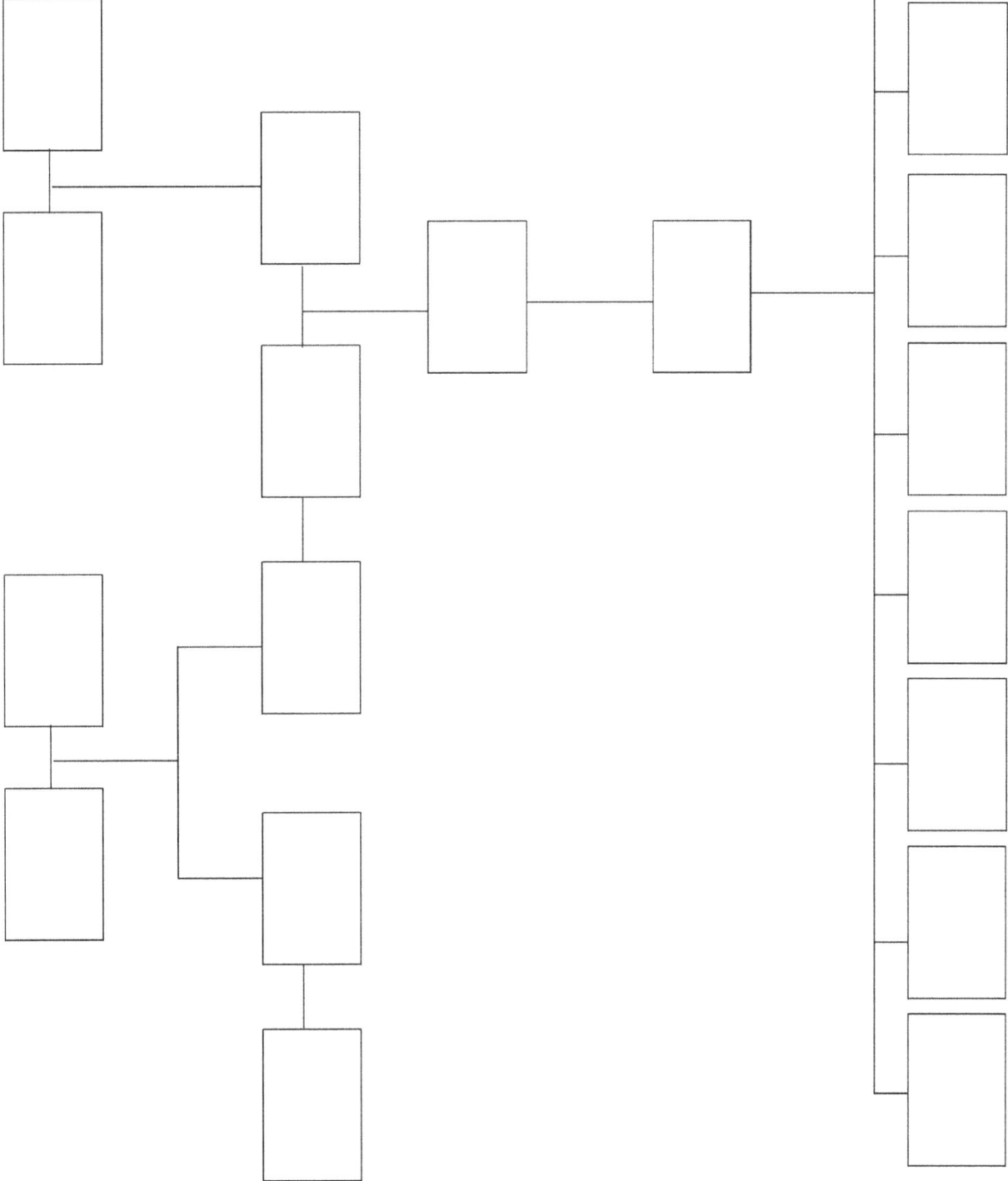

Naomi's Family Tree

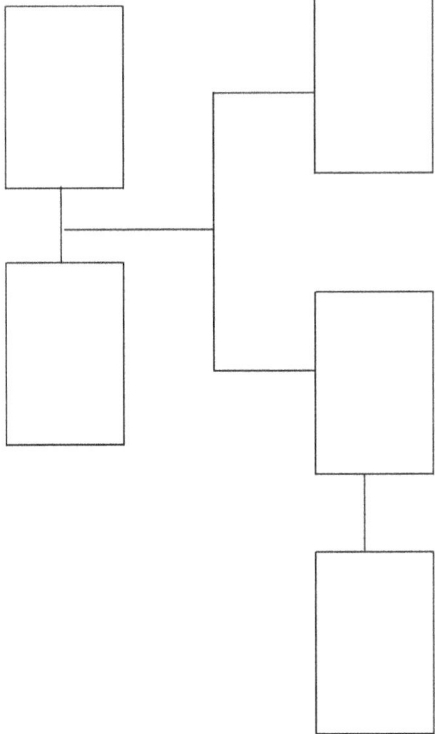

Esther

An Introduction to Esther

King Ahasuerus ruled from 486 B.C. to 465 B.C., and historically, the book of Esther takes place during part of Ahasuerus's reign. From his years of reigning, the time when Esther was written can be determined. The king had several names; those most commonly known include Ahasuerus (his Hebrew name), Xerxes (his Greek name), and Khshayarshan (his Persian name).

Esther has two names that are mentioned in this book: Esther and Hadassah. *Esther* means "star," and *Hadassah* means "myrtle." Myrtle is a plant that symbolizes peace, sweetness, and prosperity.

The festival of Purim, which was established in Esther chapter 9, is a time of remembrance, feasting, sending food to others, giving gifts, and celebrating. This special two-day holiday, which is a time of celebrating God's faithfulness, is commemorated every year among the Jewish people. The word *Purim* is derived from the word "lot" in Esther 3:7 and Esther 9:26.

Throughout the book of Esther, God's providential hand can be seen working in the lives of His people, the Jews. Psalm 121:4 says, *"Behold, He who keeps Israel Shall neither slumber nor sleep."* How true this verse is! God not only took care and watched over His people, but He bestowed amazing, wonderful blessings upon the Jewish people. He loved them and protected them—even when the story seemed bleak. When the times were unsure, God had full control.

Esther 1 and 2

*"May the L*ORD* bless you and keep you;*
*The L*ORD* make His face shine upon you*
And be gracious to you;
*The L*ORD* lift up His countenance upon you,*
And give you peace."
(Numbers 6:24-26)

Day One

Esther

What lessons the book of Esther has for us! I know I have learned a great many lessons from the life of Esther, including how to intercede on the behalf of others, how God intervenes in the lives of the believers, how God has His way in our life and nothing is a coincidence, and how God wants only the best for you and me. That is only a short list of the many lessons to be learned! God has numerous lessons in store for us to learn during these next five weeks. Spend time asking Him to open your heart to learn what He has for you to discover. Be receptive to receive what He is teaching you!

1. Before you start today's lesson, read through the book of Esther. As you are reading, ask the Lord to show you exactly what He wants you to learn while you are reading through this book. What is the Lord showing you? What is the main theme of Esther?

2. You will notice as you work through the book of Esther that God's name is not mentioned. Even though the name of Jesus isn't directly mentioned, we can still see His hand throughout the entire book. We may not hear directly from Him, but we can sense His constant presence. Verses in the Bible show us we do not have to see Him to know that He is with us. Write out the following verses:

    Psalm 97:6

Psalm 98:2, 3

1 Peter 1:8

2 Corinthians 9:7

3. God set in place strict requirements for the nation of Israel in Deuteronomy 28:1, 2, 8, and 10. The Hebrew people needed to follow these rules in order to receive His blessing on their lives and their country. What were the requirements?

4. King Xerxes' banquet celebrated what event that had occurred?

5. The king's banquet was nothing short of extravagant. What does this lavishness imply about the king, his character, his personality, his values, his rule, and his authority?

6. What exactly did the king ask Queen Vashti to do?

Vashti's issue was not one of sin but of showing disrespect toward her husband. King

Ahasuerus' pride had been hurt because his wife had disrespected him in front of his officials. Men place a great value on respect. Ahasuerus' anger boiled because Vashti refused to come when he had called for her. He knew that she had no respect for him.

In the last verse of Ephesians 5, God instructed the wife to respect her husband, and the husband is to love his wife. When God gave these instructions, He knew exactly what each gender needed: the husband needs his wife's respect; the wife needs her husband's love. What an important lesson to learn before you are married and one to keep putting into practice after you are married.

"Nevertheless let each one of you in particular so love his own wife as himself, and let the wife see that she respects her husband" (Ephesians 5:33).

7. Though we are not given a reason as to why Vashti refused Xerxes' request, Titus 2:5 clearly describes what would have been the best response.

The reason for King Xerxes's anger is clearly revealed: pride. His pride was the root of the issue when Vashti refused to come at his call. Pride has a way of making people do things they would not normally do, such as declaring that Vashti would never again be allowed in the king's presence.

Pride is never a character trait of which to be proud. Once pride seeps into our lives, we open the door to practices that would be out of character for us. As a Christian, we will face pride, even on a daily basis, but we must not allow it to take hold of our life. Write a short prayer asking God to help you overcome any root of pride in your life. Be as specific as possible. He is the only One Who can help you overcome pride.

Webster's Dictionary describes *pride* as "a high or inordinate opinion of one's own dignity, importance, merit, or superiority, whether as cherished in the mind or as displayed in bearing, conduct, etc."

8. Do you think the wise men gave the king the best advice? How could the advice have been better?

9. I hope that memorizing the verses is getting easier each week! I find memorization is easier for me by not only saying the verse out loud but by writing it down a few times. Quote the verse out loud a few times before writing it down. Hopefully, you will establish a method that makes memorizing the easiest for you.

   Write Numbers 6:24-26 to help you know the verse by the end of the week.

Day Two

Have you ever made a rash decision based on your emotional state at the time? Did you regret your hasty choice? King Ahasuerus surely did!

His anger over Vashti's refusal to come at his beck and call caused him to take an action he would later regret. In the same way, we can make harsh decisions which are based on an emotion we are feeling. The king's decision was based on his anger.

"A man who isolates himself seeks his own desire; He rages against all wise judgment. [2]A fool has no delight in understanding, but in expressing his own heart" (Proverbs 18:1, 2).

Don't forget to start your day in prayer! Also, ask the Lord to help you make wise decisions, and when the emotions are rising high, seek Him for help with making the correct decision.

1. Describe and explain what Esther 1:10 means.

2. Open up the Bible to see what God has to say about being in *"high spirits"* or "to be drunk." After reading each of the following verses, write down the verse under the correct reference.

   Hosea 4:11

   Proverbs 20:1

Ephesians 5:18

Time and time again in the book of Esther, King Xerxes consulted his magicians and astrologers to seek their wisdom. The Bible shows us what we should do concerning this issue. God is the only One Who truly knows the future. He is the One Who is in control of every aspect of our life.

Isaiah 44:25, *"Who frustrates the signs of the babblers, and drivers diviners mad; who turns wise men backward and makes their knowledge foolishness."*

Daniel 5:15, *"Now the wise men, the astrologers, have been brought in before me, that they should read this writing and make known to me its interpretation, but they could not give the interpretation of the thing."*

As you can see from these two scriptural examples, only God can show us what to do in every circumstance and situation.

3. Though very little is known of King Artaxerxes at this point, what are some of his character qualities?

4. How did Vashti's actions affect all the women in the kingdom?

5. Do you agree with the king's banishment of Queen Vashti for not appearing when he called for her? Why or why not?

Historically, Persian law was irrevocable. Once a law was set in place, not even the king himself could change or revoke the law. Knowing these facts makes me think that any king would need to be careful regarding the advice he accepted, and how he set the law in motion.

At the same time, knowing this process makes me excited! It shows me how God is already working, and preparing the way for Esther to walk in His ways.

6. Who was to become the ruler in his own home?

7. How is the husband's being the ruler of the home in line with what the Bible says? How does the husband's being the head of the home correlate with Christ and the church? Use Ephesians 5:22-33 and 1 Corinthians 11:3 as your guide. If you find a diagram helpful, draw one to illustrate their correlation.

Day Three

"Charm is deceitful and beauty is passing, but a woman who fears the Lord, she shall be praised" (Proverbs 31:30).

Esther possessed a true inner beauty, which came from a heart that sought after God. Esther's inward beauty radiated from her personality and her walk with the Lord. I can only wonder what it was that drew King Ahasuerus to Esther, but I can only think that her inward beauty could have been the attribute that the king noticed. I am sure something made her quite different from the other girls.

Ask God to instill in you an inner beauty that will shine for Him. Others will be able to see this beauty and recognize that you are different because of who you are—the person who God has made you to be.

1. Only one qualification was required for the beautiful, young women King Xerxes wanted brought to the palace. What qualification did they need to meet?

2. How did King Xerxes decide who would be his queen?

3. Esther and Mordecai were both from the same tribe. From which tribe of Israel did they descend?

Mordecai's great-grandfather, Kish, was a member of the Jewish people who experienced the Babylon deportation, which happened when Babylon fell to Medo-Persia in 539 B.C. Kish came from the tribe of Benjamin, and the Benjamite tribe can be traced back to Saul's father in 1,100 B.C. Mordecai was in the fourth generation of the deported Jews.

4. Esther was the future queen's Persian name. What is her Hebrew name mentioned in verse 7?

5. Did you know that we are all adopted children of the King? What a wonderful thought! Once a person accepts Christ into his heart, God adopts that new believer into His family. Read Ephesians 1:5 and explain what the verse means to you.

6. Setting a good example is extremely important. People should be able to see that we are Christians by the way we live. Esther perfectly modeled setting a good example, so much so that Hegai was impressed by her demeanor. Likewise, we should also strive to be good examples. Proverbs 3:3, 4 describes the example Esther set and what happened in her life because she let her character shine through. Using a New Living Translation, fill in the following blanks:

   "Never let _____ and _____ leave you! Tie them around your neck as a _____. Write them _____ within your heart. [4]Then you will find favor with both God and people, and you will earn a _____ _____ " (Proverbs 3:3, 4 NLT).

7. God is the One Who numbers our days. He is the One Who allows us to prosper. He is the One Who exalts His people. He is the One Who blesses His people. Esther is an exemplary example of one whom God has exalted and blessed. Describe the promises that are found in Psalm 75:6, 7. What do you learn about God's characteristics from these verses?

8. God has given all of us unique experiences, blessings, and opportunities. What are some of those He has given you? How did He bless you with them? How did you use them?

Day Four

What kind of woman do you want to be remembered as? What kind of character do you display? Esther displayed a virtuous character; something intangible about her stood out, and the king noticed.

I want to be the type of woman in whom others see a difference—one, because I'm a Christian, and two, because I want to be a woman of virtue. John MacArthur writes, "True holiness and virtue command permanent respect and affection, far more than charm and beauty of face and form."[9]

Ask the Lord to allow your light and character as a Christian woman to shine brightly in this generation. Ask the Lord to use you in ways that you could never imagine. Shine brightly for Him!

1. Place yourself in Esther's shoes. What would you have done regarding keeping your ethnicity a secret from everyone?

Proverbs 13:3 describes what Esther did in her predicament with keeping her heritage a secret: *"Those who guard their lips preserve their lives, but those who speak rashly will come to ruin"* (NIV).

"The integrity of the upright guides them, but the unfaithful are destroyed by their duplicity" (Proverbs 11:3 NIV).

2. What does this chapter teach you about Who God is?

3. What additional background information does Esther 2:1-7 reveal about who Mordecai is?

4. Character is important! Character is who you are when no one is watching you. Esther is already showing her great character and wisdom. She listened to her elders regarding keeping her heritage hidden, but Proverbs gives us an example of what happens when we do or do not submit to instruction. Record what the following verses imply as your Bible says.

   Proverbs 15:5

   Proverbs 9:13

   Proverbs 13:3

5. Esther 2:12 explains the beauty treatments that purified each young woman who was a possible candidate for the throne. Write down what the treatments contained.

Unfortunately, King Ahasuerus was not the only king who followed the practice of having more than one woman. Only one woman could be named as the queen; the others were considered concubines since they were not married to the king. King David and King Solomon also had concubines. "Not only did many of the girls feel used and rejected, but they faced a life of 'perpetual widowhood' as a concubine, unable to ever enjoy the kindness of a faithful husband or the chance to raise a normal family."[10]

When Esther was taken to the palace with the other women, she knew that ultimately she could become one of the king's concubines and remain in the palace until her death. However, God had extensive plans in mind, which included making her queen.

I cannot even begin to imagine how the nation would have survived without Esther's willingness and Mordecai's being used by God. Esther, not knowing the future, trusted that God would only use her life for His good. One of my favorite authors, Corrie Ten Boom, wisely stated, "Never be afraid to trust an unknown future to a known God."[11] Though Miss Ten Boom wrote this axiom centuries later, Esther had already trusted God and had lived out the truth of this quote. She came to know the depth of the meaning of this truth.

I pray that you will do the same with your life—that you will trust your unknown future to a loving God Who knows your future.

6. Wise Esther once again chose to obey her authority rather than make her own decision regarding her outfit for her night with the king. Hegai advised Esther on what to wear. He knew that her inward beauty would shine through without the outward embellishment of fancy clothing. Precious lady, our inward beauty is far more important to God than our outward beauty. The Old and New Testaments both tell what God thinks regarding our beauty. According to the following Scriptures, what does God think?

   1 Samuel 16:8

1 Timothy 2:9, 10

1 Peter 3:3, 4

Day Five

We are now beginning to see the fruit of God's secret workings: first, with Esther's being selected as a candidate for becoming the replacement queen; second, her being chosen as the queen; third, Mordecai's being at the right place at the right time, thus saving the king's life.

To say God works in mysterious ways would be nothing short of the truth! We learned a good deal about God's using each of us for His glory!

"For we are His workmanship, created in Christ Jesus for good works, which God prepared beforehand that we should walk in them" (Ephesians 2:10).

Start the day by praying Ephesians 2:10 for your life. Thank Him that He has great works in store for you!

1. God will place authority and responsibility upon those whom He chooses. He also can take away or add someone to a powerful position. Using Psalm 75:6, 7 as a guide, write down the verses in your own words and explain what these verses mean in reference to Esther 2:16, 17.

"God ultimately raises up leaders for one primary reason: His glory. He shows His power in our weakness. He demonstrates His wisdom in our folly. We are all like a turtle on a fence post. If you walk by a fence post and see a turtle on top of it, then you know someone came by and put it there. In the same way, God gives leadership according to His good pleasure." – Matt Chandler[12]

2. Where did the king find the record of the plot to murder him?

The Hebrew words for the *book of the annals* is "the book of the matters of the day," i.e., the official court records of memorable events.

3. Who made the king aware of the tragedy to come?

4. How did Esther respect her cousin once she became queen?

Esther never lost her respect for Mordecai; it's as simple as that. Mordecai possessed great wisdom and provided guidance for Esther. She continued to respect him even after she became the queen. Respect and honor are very similar in the fact that a particular person's character is valued and esteemed. You could say that you look up to the person because of his walk with the Lord, and how that walk translates into his everyday life. According to Dictionary.com, honor and respect are defined as follows:

Honor:
- "high respect, as for worth, merit, or rank"

Respect:
- "esteem for or a sense of the worth or excellence of a person, a personal quality or ability, or something considered as a manifestation of a personal quality or ability

Esther both respected and honored Mordecai. Do you find respect and honor toward your "elders" to come easily or is it something you need to work on? Esther is a wonderful example to me of how we can respect and honor those who are over us.

Much can be gleaned from Esther's example in how she responded to Mordecai.

"A kindhearted woman gains honor…" (Proverbs 11:16 NIV).

5. What important truth did you learn this week?

6. Write a prayer to the Lord, thanking Him that He accepts us not based on appearance or talent but through His Son and what Jesus did on the cross.

7. Write down this week's memory verse.

"God is great not just because nothing is too big for Him. God is great because nothing is too small for Him, either." – Mark Batterson[13]

Esther 3 and 4

"Many are the afflictions of the righteous,
*But the L*ORD *delivers him out of them all."*
(Psalm 34:19)

Day One

Today's lesson speaks about following God's instructions and His plan for your life. His plan for your life is better than anything you could ever dream, prepare, or want for your life. The following verse addresses the promise that God has for us.

> *"For I know the thoughts that I think toward you, says the LORD, thoughts of peace and not of evil, to give you a future and a hope"* (Jeremiah 29:11).

What a wonderful plan created by a wonderful Heavenly Father! Knowing that God only wants the best for me is incredibly comforting. You are His princess. You are His child.

Thank your Heavenly Father for the comfort of this promise and be thankful that He has only the best in mind for you!

1. If you carefully read Esther 3:1, you will discover that Haman is a descendant of Agag, who was a king of the Amalekites. God instructed certain people throughout the Bible to destroy the Amalekites. When God's people listen, there will be blessings; however, when God's people disobey, a price will be paid for that disobedience. Saul is one of the men whom God commanded to put away the Amalekites. Read 1 Samuel 15 and recount how Saul chose not to follow God's plan exactly.

2. Has there been a time in your life when you haven't followed God in the specific way He instructed? What was the outcome?

3. Why do you think Haman wanted to kill all of the Jews instead of only Mordecai?

4. In verse 2, the Bible says that everyone but Mordecai knelt down to Haman. One way to pay respect to a person in those days was to bow down before him. Mordecai obeyed the Lord in this situation by fearing the Lord and not man. Acts 5:29 describes what we need to do in any situation. What does this verse mean?

Disrespected is what Haman felt when Mordecai did not bow down to him. Haman's hatred didn't simply begin with Mordecai; rather, he was disenchanted with the Jews as a nation. Haman did not want Mordecai alone to suffer the consequences of his hatred; he wanted the entire Jewish nation to suffer. His intense hatred targeted God's chosen people! *"When the righteous are in authority, the people rejoice; but when a wicked man rules, the people groan"* (Proverbs 29:2).

5. Esther 3:7 foretells the month in which the Jews will face annihilation. How long will it be from the time Haman cast lots until the day the attack on the Jews will be executed?

Haman's advisers were comprised of people who made decisions based on superstitions. These superstitions had their roots in astrology and casting lots.

I personally believe that listening to superstitions is the silliest way to make a decision. The best way is to always go before the Lord and seek His wisdom.

6. Have you learned what the Lord says about casting lots? Reading Proverbs 16:33 tells us about these lots and what God thinks about them. After reading the verse, write it down word-for-word.

The chosen month for the lot to be carried out was the month of Adar, which falls between February and March. A full eleven months would pass before the fulfillment of Haman's heinous decree would take place.

Oh, I can't wait to see how God is going to intervene!

7. Write down Psalm 34:19 to help you remember this week's memory verse.

Day Two

What does *reputation* mean? *Webster's Dictionary* provides the following meaning:

Reputation:

1. "the estimation in which a person or thing is held, especially by the community or the public generally; repute"
2. "a favorable and publicly recognized name or standing for merit, achievement, reliability, etc."

Your reputation is what people hold your character to. It is another way to judge a person.

Today's lesson will reveal the difference in the reputations of Haman, Mordecai, and Esther. Before starting today's lesson, ask the Lord to give you a reputation that others will be able to recognize the fact that you are a Christian.

1. People have tried to eliminate the Jewish race for centuries. Hitler is an example of a leader who tried to unsuccessfully destroy the Jews. God holds His people in His hand, and nothing can happen to His people unless He first allows it. God has written accounts in His Word to display this very fact. What story in the Bible is an example of that wonderful promise?

2. Ouch! Did you notice the word used to describe Haman's family line? What does that word say about their family's character?

3. Carefully read each of the following verses. Circle the words or phrases that describe Haman's reputation.

"These six things the LORD hates—yes, seven are an abomination to Him:
[17]a proud look, a lying tongue, hands that shed innocent blood,
[18]a heart that devises wicked plans, feet that are swift in running to evil,
[19]a false witness who speaks lies, and one who sows discord brethren."
(Proverbs 6:16-19)

4. What are some character traits in your life that you are proud of?

5. What attributes could use a little more work?

The Bible tell us in Galatians chapter 5 that the fruit of the Spirit is love, joy, peace, patience, kindness, goodness, faithfulness, gentleness, and self-control.

"But the fruit of the Spirit is love, joy, peace, longsuffering, kindness, goodness, faithfulness,[23]gentleness, self-control. Against such there is no law" (Galatians 5:22, 23).

We need to be daily putting these character traits into practice. However, they can only be achieved and developed when we are in the Spirit and in the Word.

Choose one of the fruit of the Spirit and, over the next few weeks, pray for that one to become a fruit in your life. See how God is faithful to help you begin to establish your choice in your life.

6. Three words are used to describe what Haman planned to do to the Jews: *destroy, kill* and *annihilate*. Such strong words! If you will continue reading verse 13, you will see that the decree applied to all of the Jews—men, women, and children—the young and the old. Haman wanted the Jews destroyed in one day. Look up the three words in the dictionary and write down their definition.

Destroy:

Kill:

Annihilate:

7. Our actions will show when we truly trust God with everything. When we trust God, we will respond differently than expected to the situation at hand. Read James 2:26. How can we trust God more and more?

Day Three

Prayer

The power of prayer is huge! Prayer has an incredible amount of need in our lives.

"I have joyfully dedicated my whole life to the object of exemplifying how much may be accomplished by prayer and faith." – George Müller[14]

George Müller, who is one my Christian heroes, was known as a great man of faith and prayer. George started an orphanage for the parentless children of Bristol. One thing about George inspires me is that he prayed fervently and with faith the size of a mustard seed.

Müller never asked anyone for money nor told anyone of his needs, yet God always provided—whether it was breakfast for the children or money for different necessities. God brought in millions of dollars through one man's prayer.[15]

We can do so much through prayer! Don't ever underestimate the power of prayer and asking God for what you need! Spend time today asking God for things that have not yet come to pass and ask Him with faith the size of a mustard seed!

1. Mordecai's example continues to amaze me. He keeps showing us the importance of following the Lord in every circumstance. Mordecai's character and conduct show us how He truly follows the Lord. What lessons can we learn from the life of Mordecai?

"When Mordecai learned all that had happened, he tore his clothes and put on sackcloth and ashes, and went out into the midst of the city. He cried out with a loud and bitter cry. ²He went as far as the front of the king's gate, for no one might enter the king's gate clothed with sackcloth. ³And in every province where the king's command and decree arrived, there was great mourning among the Jews, with fasting, weeping, and wailing; and many lay in sackcloth and ashes" (Esther 4:1-3).

Mordecai's first response to the decree was to tear his clothes and put on sackcloth and ashes. *Sackcloth* is constructed from "coarse, black cloth that comes from goat's hair." Normally, sackcloth is accompanied by ashes. The importance of ashes and sackcloth is twofold: as a sign of repentance and as a prayer for deliverance.

2. Record how sackcloth and ashes were used in each of the following references: 1) for repentance or 2) for deliverance.

    1 Kings 21:25-27

    Nehemiah 9:1-3

    2 Kings 19:1-2

    Matthew 11:21

Daniel 9:3

Job 42:1-6

3. God has taken me places in my life where I would not have gone unless He led me there. He directed my steps like He led Esther into the path He had for her. We may think that God has us in a specific place for one particular reason, but unbeknown to us, we could be there for an entirely different reason. What do the following verses teach about the Lord's leading?

Proverbs 16:4

Proverbs 16:19

4. Mordecai's peace came from a promise that God had made long before to Abraham in Genesis 17:1-21. God made a forever, unconditional promise to the nation of Israel. God has never failed to keep His promise to His children. Why would He begin to fail His children at this time? Mordecai trusted God for his life and with his future. He trusted God to keep His promise.

Write out Leviticus 26:44 and Romans 8:31.

5. Fill in the blanks: "Many are the_____ of the _____, but the _____ _____ him out of them all" (Psalm 34:19).

6. Read Jehoshaphat's prayer in 2 Chronicles 20:5-12. In what ways is this a model prayer for any child of God who is in trouble?

7. What key details did Mordecai know about Haman's evil plot against the Jews?

8. What important truth did you learn from today's lesson?

"The fear of the LORD is the instruction of wisdom, and before honor is humility."
(Proverbs 15:33)

Day Four

Courage

One character trait Esther would need to save her people was courage. I believe that God placed her in this position for very task of saving her people. Esther would need to be courageous and brave in order to face the king since he had not called for her. Charles Spurgeon once said, "You have been wishing for another position where you could do something for Jesus: do not wish anything of the kind, but serve Him where you are."[16] How very true! God will use you in the place you are in right now.

"Courage is not the absence of fear, but rather the assessment that something else is more important than fear." – Franklin D. Roosevelt[17]

1. Think about a time when God used you specifically where you were. What was the outcome of being led by the Lord to His place of desiring to use you?

2. God uses ordinary people to do extraordinary things! Isn't that a wonderful thought?! After reading the following verses, describe how they were used in a remarkable way.

   - Daniel (Daniel 6)

   - Mary, the mother of Jesus (Luke 1:46-55)

• Joseph (Genesis 37:39-47)

• Nehemiah (Nehemiah 1-3)

3. Philippians 1:21 would have encouraged Esther in her time of prayer and fasting. Esther really understood in later chapters what it meant to live for Christ with the possibility of being at death's door. Write out the following verses:

Philippians 1:21

Matthew 10:28

4. Do you know what it means to fast? Esther undoubtedly understood the importance of fasting and praying. *Fasting* is "denying your body of something it wants and filling it with the Word of God." What are some things in your life that you could fast over?

Another definition of *fasting* is "denying yourself of something in the flesh and focusing on our spiritual growth, prayer and reading the Bible." A side of fasting also addresses seeking the Lord and His will for your life.

Esther, Mordecai, and the Jews fasted and prayed to seek the Lord's favor regarding the edict that Haman had set in place, knowing this edict would completely wipe out the Jews. The Lord heard their cries, and later chapters record exactly how He answered their prayers.

"But those who wait on the Lord shall renew their strength; they shall mount up with wings like eagles, they shall run and not be weary, they shall walk and not faint" (Isaiah 40:31).

5. Quite a few instances in the Bible address the matter of God's people praying and fasting. It will be wonderful to see the outcome of how He will answer our prayers. The answer may not be right away, as Daniel discovered, but God will surely answer His people. After reading Daniel 10, answer the following questions pertaining to the story.

   • How long did it take the angel to deliver his message to Daniel?

   • What happened to the messenger on his way to talk with Daniel?

   • Daniel 10:2 records that Daniel did not eat certain foods while he was fasting. What types of food did he refrain from eating?

6. Jesus also describes how our prayer and fasting should appear. Using Matthew 6:16-18 as your guide, circle any key words.

"And when you fast, don't make it obvious, as the hypocrites do, for they try to look miserable and disheveled so people will admire them for their fasting. I tell you the truth, that is the only reward they will ever get. [17]But when you fast, comb your hair and wash your face. [18]Then no one will notice that you are fasting, except your Father, who knows what you do in private. And your Father, who sees everything, will reward you" (Matthew 6:16-18 NLT)

Day Five

"...because there is no other God who can deliver like this" (Daniel 3:29).

How true! Only God can deliver us from all of our fears, trials, worries, and doubts. We have been seeing this very fact come true in Esther's life, and we will continue to see how the Lord delivers His children.

"Trust in the LORD with all your heart, and lean not on your own understanding; ⁶In all your ways acknowledge Him, and He shall direct your paths" (Proverbs 3:5, 6).

1. How is the queen's statement in Esther 4:16, *"...if I perish, I perish"* similar to the story of Shadrach, Meshach, and Abednego in Daniel 3? What kind of stand did they take against King Nebuchadnezzar?

2. Paul faced many situations that placed his life in danger; these situations may have gotten Paul killed. Summarize the trials Paul faced under the corresponding verses:

   2 Corinthians 11:23-28

   Acts 9:28-30

Acts 20:22-24

Acts 24:1

The rationale behind the king's extending the golden scepter toward those who approached him was to protect his life. The king would only extend the scepter to those he knew and to those with whom he chose to visit. This practice protected a king's life from those who would want to harm him.

3. God has so much that He wants every believer to learn! What better women to learn from than Esther and Ruth?! Write down what you have been learning and what God has been teaching you this week.

One of my favorite verses in Esther is found in this week's chapter: Esther 4:14, *"...Yet who knows whether you have come to the kingdom for such a time as this?"*

The reason for this Scripture's being one of my favorites is that God purposefully plans every aspect of your life and mine. Nothing—nothing with God is ever coincidental. He has Ecclesiastes 3:1 in mind: *"To everything there is a season, A time for every purpose under heaven."* God literally has a reason and a plan for everything He allows.

The definition of *coincidence* according to Dictionary.com is "a striking occurrence of two or more events at one time apparently by mere chance."

By this definition, I believe we can more than sum up that Esther's being queen is nothing short of God's providence in her life, and the Jews will soon find out.

Likewise, God also has great plan in store for you! Bloom right where He has planted you. You don't know why He has you exactly where you are, but I can tell you it is for a reason. Allow Him to use you as He did Esther. He wants to! You simply need to be a willing vessel ready for God's use.

Charles Spurgeon, one of England's most well-known preachers, spoke these wise words in the nineteenth century: "You have been wishing for another position where you could do something for Jesus: do not wish anything of the kind, but serve him where you are."[18] I encourage you to do exactly what Mr. Spurgeon is suggesting! Serve the Lord exactly where He has placed you. He has great and mighty things in store for you!

4. Write a simple prayer to the Lord, asking Him to give you the boldness to grow right where you are and to allow Him to use you as an example or encouragement in the life of another. Thank Him that He is choosing to use you and for the wonderful plans He has in store for you.

5. Do you have your verse memorized? It's the last day of the week, go ahead and write down the verse that you committed to memory this week.

Esther 5 and 6

"But I will honor those who honor me."

(1 Samuel 2:30 NLT)

Day One

Esther chose to lay down her life for her people. She did not know what the outcome would be when she approached the king. Trusting God had prepared for her *"...such a time as this,"* Esther proceeded with boldness. Placing the future of her people on her shoulders, Esther went before the king. Christ performed a similar selfless act; He willingly placed our sins upon Himself. If Christ had not died for us, we would be forever lost like the Jews would have been had they not had Esther as their intercessor.

1. Before you start this new week of study, read chapters 5 and 6 of Esther and write a few sentences of summary on each chapter.

2. How do Proverbs 21:1-2 and Proverbs 16:1 show us that God is in control of everything?

3. Esther had an inward peace and a trust that can only be present because of the Lord. Esther placed every part of herself in His hands. She trusted Him completely, allowing Him to use her in amazing ways.
    Write a prayer asking the Lord to make you attentive to the specific plans He has for you in your life.

"Be anxious for nothing, but in everything by prayer and supplication, with thanksgiving, let your requests be made known to God; [7]and the peace of God, which surpasses all understanding, will guard your hearts and minds through Christ Jesus." (Philippians 4:6, 7)

4. Why do you think Esther waited until the second meeting to ask the king for her request?

5. What risk does Esther take in chapter five?

Haman's frustration toward Mordecai was drawn out from his own insecurities. We all have issues in our life that reflect on our insecurities. Every person will vary, but a few might be untrusting, shy, or fearful. Our security should come from Christ and Christ alone.

6. What are some of your insecurities?

7. Have you asked God to help you overcome your insecurities?

8. Compose a prayer to God, asking Him and allowing Him to work a work in your life to change those insecurities.

You were made in God's image. You are valued. You are beautiful. You are radiant. You are loved. You are a child of the King. You are His princess.

"I will be a Father to you, and you shall be My sons and daughters," Says the LORD Almighty" (2 Corinthians 6:18).

"The LORD has appeared of old to me, saying: "Yes, I have loved you with an everlasting love; Therefore with lovingkindness I have drawn you" (Jeremiah 31:3).

A definition of *insecurity*:

> 1. "a lack of confidence or assurance; self-doubt"

A definitions of *confidence*:

> 1. "full trust; belief in the powers, trustworthiness, or reliability of a person or thing"
>
> 2. "belief in oneself and one's powers or abilities; self-confidence; self-reliance; assurance"

God has created you to be one of His beautiful, confident daughters—confident in who Christ has made you and one who seeks Him wholeheartedly.

The woman God wants you to become is the one described in the previous sentence. She is confident in Christ, possesses a self-image that is valued in Christ, and maintains a spiritually healthy walk.

9. What advice did Haman's friends and family give to him? Would you consider the advice that Haman received as helpful or as hurtful?

My dear friend, the advice that Haman received was nothing short of harmful to him. Have you ever asked a friend for advice, knowing the person would give you the advice you wanted to hear—not the advice you truly needed? Sadly, in his hatred, Haman did exactly that: he sought the advice he wanted to hear. The advice he accepted led to his death. Psalm 1:1 describes exactly what Haman chose not to do:

> *"Blessed is the man who walks not in the counsel of the ungodly, nor stands in the path of sinners, nor sits in the seat of the scornful."*

Haman should have sought Godly counsel—not the ungodly counsel he received and followed. Another verse that Haman lived out is Ecclesiastes 10:12, 13:

> *"Words from the mouth of a wise man are gracious, but fools are consumed by their own lips. [13]At the beginning their words are folly; at the end they are wicked madness"* (NIV).

I trust that when you ask for advice that you will seek it from those who follow the Lord and seek His will for your life. Those kind of friends will have only your best interest in mind. They will want to direct you in the right direction. The following verses will help you for when you are seeking guidance:

> *"A wise man will hear and increase learning, and a man of understanding will attain wise counsel"* (Proverbs 1:5).

> *"The fear of the LORD is the beginning of knowledge…"* (Proverbs 1:7).

> *"If any of you lacks wisdom, let him ask of God, who gives to all liberally and without reproach, and it will be given to him"* (James 1:5).

10. Write down this week's verse.

"The soul was made for God, and nothing but God can fill it and make it happy." – Adam Clarke[19]

Day Two

Patience

Do you see patience as perhaps being a difficult character trait to learn? I know I do! It's one of the fruit of the Spirit, but we can attain this discipline with God's help.

I do not know anyone who has never had to work on having patience. Andrew Murray says it perfectly:

> "Give God His glory by resting in Him, by trusting Him fully, by waiting patiently for Him. This patience honours Him greatly. It leaves Him, as God on the throne, to do His work. It yields self wholly into His hands. It lets God be God."[20]

A few years back, I asked the Lord to help me work on patience. I know, "Who asks for *that*?"! Anyway, I did. I learned many lessons, and gaining more patience was anything but easy, I can tell you that! One aspect to my learning this lesson was placing a black vinyl script sticker above my bed that said, "Love is patient" from 1 Corinthians 13. I wanted to have a daily reminder instructing me of the need to exercise patience every single day. *"Love is patient…."* When I am being patient, then I am displaying love as well.

As difficult as it is to speak, ask the Lord to teach you to have a heart that displays patience in every circumstance. Seek His will, which includes having patience in waiting upon the Lord, having patience in His perfect plan, and having patience in your current situation.

1. Look up Ephesians 1:6, and write down what the verse says.

2. List the differences between the character of Mordecai and Haman.

3. In difficult situations, how can you react with courage and kindness?

4. How high were the gallows Haman had built for Mordecai to die on?

"A pointed stake is set upright in the ground and the culprit is taken, placed on the sharp point, and then pulled down the legs till the stake that went in at the fundament passes up through the body and comes out through the neck. A most dreadful species of punishment, in which revenge and cruelty may glut the utmost of their malice. The culprit lives a considerable time in excruciating agonies." – Adam Clarke[21]

Patience is a fruit of the Spirit that God wants every believer to exercise on a consistent basis. Exhibit patience when co-workers aren't reacting well to a situation. Display patience when you are in the middle of a trial, and you cannot see the end. Demonstrate patience with your prayer requests.

Patience requires practice, and practice makes progress. The more you work at patience, the better you will be at making this discipline a habit.

I know for many years I prayed for the Lord to instill in me a spirit of patience. Be careful what you ask for! The Lord gave me that and much more. I have learned through having seven siblings what patience means. I have learned through serving at church what patience means.

Patience isn't simply holding out for something you want. And yes, patience is more than waiting; patience is also having a loss of temper. Allow me to explain. When one of my siblings does something that would normally provoke a spirit that is filled with anger, I ask the Lord to instill in me a spirit that pours out patience.

One lesson I have learned is that patience can never be perfected, but God can help us practice patience in everyday situations. Remember "practice makes progress!"

> "Rejoicing in hope, patient in tribulation, continuing steadfastly in prayer" (Romans 12:12).

> "With all lowliness and gentleness, with longsuffering, bearing with one another in love," (Ephesians 4:2).

> "So then, my beloved brethren, let every man be swift to hear, slow to speak, slow to wrath" (James 1:19).

> "A wrathul man stirs up strife, but he who is slow to anger allays contention" (Proverbs 15:18).

5. We all have times when we do not want to exercise patience. Write a prayer to the Lord asking Him to help you with patience this week.

6. How did Esther intercede on the behalf of her people? What does *Intercede* mean?

7. Romans 8:26 and 27 have much to teach us about intercession. What are a few of the lessons that these verses teach about how intercession works and who intercedes on our behalf?

8. Read Exodus 32:7-14. Why did Moses intercede for the people of Israel in this passage? What happened as a result?

9. In what ways can you intercede on the behalf of others?

Day Three

Haman was quick to answer when King Ahasuerus asked what he would do to honor someone. Immediately thinking the honor was for him, he made some elaborate suggestions, including wearing the king's royal robe and his crown, riding the king's horse, and being paraded on horseback through the city. Because Haman was desperate to be honored throughout all the land, he unwittingly placed himself in a position he was not to receive.

Proverbs 18:12, *"Before destruction the heart of a man is haughty, and before honor is humility."* Haman's pride came before humility. His heart longed to be in a place where he would be number-one.

1. Other instances in the Bible where pride led people do wicked things can be found in the following verses. Read each verse and write down a lesson that can be learned from each instance.

   Isaiah 14:14

   Exodus 5:2

   2 Kings 20:13-18

2. Pride has a way of getting the best of us. Many Bible verses clearly state what will happen when we allow pride into our lives. Write down a few word of summary for each verse.

Galatians 6:3

Proverbs 26:12

Romans 12:16

James 4:6

Proverbs 27:2

3. In concluding this lesson on pride, how does the Lord see our pride? What does pride do to us?

Definitions of *pride*:

1. "a high or inordinate opinion of one's own dignity, importance, merit, or superiority, whether as cherished in the mind or as displayed in bearing, conduct, etc. "

2. "the state or feeling of being proud"

3. "a becoming or dignified sense of what is due to oneself or one's position or character; self-respect; self-esteem"

A definition of *humility*:

1. "the quality or condition of being humble; modest opinion or estimate of one's own importance, rank, etc."

4. Esther trusted God with her life! Daniel 3 tells of three men who were ready to lay down their life for God when He stepped in and performed a miracle. Read the following verses and draw a circle around God's name every time you see it.

Then Nebuchadnezzar was full of fury, and the expression on his face changed toward Shadrach, Meshach, and Abed-Nego. He spoke and commanded that they heat the furnace seven times more than it was usually heated. [20]*And he commanded certain mighty men of valor who were in his army to bind Shadrach, Meshach, and Abed-Nego, and cast them into the burning fiery furnace.* [21]*Then these men were bound in their coats, their trousers, their turbans, and their other garments, and were cast into the midst of the burning fiery furnace.* [22]*Therefore, because the king's command was urgent, and the furnace exceedingly hot, the flame of the fire killed those men who took up Shadrach, Meshach, and Abed-Nego.* [23]*And these three men, Shadrach, Meshach, and Abed-Nego, fell down bound into the midst of the burning fiery furnace.*

[24]*Then King Nebuchadnezzar was astonished; and he rose in haste and spoke, saying to his counselors, "Did we not cast three men bound into the midst of the fire?"*

They answered and said to the king, "True, O king." ²⁵

"Look!" he answered, "I see four men loose, walking in the midst of the fire; and they are not hurt, and the form of the fourth is like the Son of God."

²⁶Then Nebuchadnezzar went near the mouth of the burning fiery furnace and spoke, saying, "Shadrach, Meshach, and Abed-Nego, servants of the Most High God, come out, and come here." Then Shadrach, Meshach, and Abed-Nego came from the midst of the fire. ²⁷And the satraps, administrators, governors, and the king's counselors gathered together, and they saw these men on whose bodies the fire had no power; the hair of their head was not singed nor were their garments affected, and the smell of fire was not on them.

²⁸Nebuchadnezzar spoke, saying, "Blessed be the God of Shadrach, Meshach, and Abed-Nego, who sent His Angel and delivered His servants who trusted in Him, and they have frustrated the king's word, and yielded their bodies, that they should not serve nor worship any god except their own God! ²⁹Therefore I make a decree that any people, nation, or language which speaks anything amiss against the God of Shadrach, Meshach, and Abed-Nego shall be cut in pieces, and their houses shall be made an ash heap; because there is no other God who can deliver like this" (Daniel 3:19-29).

5. Did anything specific stand out as you read this account in Daniel 3? What did you learn about how the Lord works in our lives? Be detailed in your explanation.

Day Four

Once again, you will see God's providential hand at work in the life of Mordecai. God's being at work is somewhat of normality in the book of Esther, but don't discount its importance.

Keep your eyes peeled, your ears open, and your mind ready to receive the wonderful treasures that God has in store for you today as you dig deep into the lives of His people.

Seek Him and His heart wholeheartedly today! Allow Him to show you the nugget of truth that He has in store for you!

"And you will seek Me and find Me, when you search for Me with all your heart" (Jeremiah 29:13).

1. How did the king find out about the assassination plot?

Five years had passed since the incident of Mordecai's saving the king occurred. I cannot help but think that Mordecai thought he would never be rewarded, especially after the length of time that had passed. Knowing the character of Mordecai, I believe the reason why he revealed the assassination plot was not to be rewarded; rather, he wished to save a life.

You may think that no one sees what you do. My friend, don't worry; God sees you and He is proud of you for making the right decisions—even though making the right choice is not always the easiest.

2. Upon who would you place the blame for the king's sleepless night? Of what importance is this incident?

3. What promise does Malachi 3:16 hold for those who fear the Lord?

What a wonderful promise that we, as believers, have in our future! His promise tells us that He will listen to those who fear Him and honor His name.

4. What situation happens in Esther 6 that shows God's hand at work?

5. In what way does King Xerxes respond to how Mordecai helped thwart the assassination plan?

6. What were the honors that Haman described to the king in verses 7 through 9?

"Therefore the LORD God of Israel says: 'I said indeed that your house and the house of your father would walk before Me forever.' But now the LORD says: 'Far be it from Me; for those who honor Me I will honor, and those who despise Me shall be lightly esteemed' " (1 Samuel 2:30).

"If anyone serves Me, let him follow Me; and where I am, there My servant will be also. If anyone serves Me, him My Father will honor" (John 12:26).

Haman was too quick to assume. Instead of displaying humility, he immediately became proud. I can hear him saying, "Why wouldn't the king want to honor *me*? There isn't anyone else who should be honored more than me. It's about time that he publicly showed his gratitude for all that I have done for him."

I cringe when I see the amount of humble pie that Haman was served. No one likes to be humbled. However, humility is a character trait of great importance. Esther 6:12 tells of the shame and embarrassment that Haman felt when he learned that Mordecai was the one to be honored.

Oh, the wisdom that can be gained if you will follow Proverbs 16:18 more carefully! *"Pride goes **before** destruction, and a haughty spirit **before** a fall."* As you can see, I bolded the word *before* because *before* you can be humbled, you must have a spirit of pride. Pride and a haughty spirit precede the fall or destruction.

7. Before you answer this question, re-read the previous section and really think about humility. After pondering what Proverbs 16:18 means, write down a couple of ways that you can apply this verse to your own life.

I know that for myself, I would rather read the Bible to see how people made mistakes and learn from their mistakes. Experience is not the best teacher; someone else's experience is! The Bible gives us the good, the bad, and the ugly. One example is King David:

The *good*: God helped him to defeat the Philistine giant, Goliath.

The *bad*: The people are numbered, and a terrible disease resulted.

The *ugly*: An adulterous affair with Bathsheba leads to killing Uriah and their firstborn dying.

I encourage you to use the Bible as your guide for your life. If you do, you will be spared much grief and heartache later on.

Day Five

God is detail-orientated. He plans and prepares each step before we walk in it. He plans a step; He plans a day. Each one is special, and the Lord directs each one. Proverbs 16:9 tells us: *"A man's heart plans his way, but the LORD directs his steps."* This truth will become a reality in Esther chapter 6.

In wrapping up chapters 5 and 6 of Esther for this week, I pray that we have taken the lessons that Esther has taught us to heart. A wise woman will listen to instruction—even if the instruction came from centuries ago. I pray that you will become a wise woman who learns from others' mistakes as ones to avoid on her own. I also pray that you will have had your faith increased in knowing that God is truly at work in our life—even when we do not see His hand right away.

Start your day in prayer by telling the Lord of your desire to know Him more and more. Thank Him for the work going on in your life even when you don't understand exactly why He is doing what He is.

1. As you read Daniel 4:28-37, you will see some similarities between King Nebuchadnezzar and Haman. List a few of the similarities that you notice.

Haman and Nebuchadnezzar are similar in the way that they placed others into a position that only God should have. Their pride became their idol. They loved the attention and praise they received. Haman and Nebuchadnezzar relished the praise and allowed that pride to become their focus.

It's so easy to allow pride into our life.

Haman was ultimately killed because of his pride. Nebuchadnezzar lived like a farm animal for several years.

2. We all have areas of our life that we need to surrender to the Lord. Surrendering takes place when we recognize that not only can we not do it without the Lord, but our laying down the issues that we have is required. Our surrender allows the Lord to take full control of the intimate aspects of our life.

Think of a few areas that you can fully surrender to the Lord. Before you write them down, ask Him if there is anything that you haven't fully surrendered to Him that you need to.

I know for myself that I do not realize how tightly I am holding onto certain areas until I seek the Lord and ask Him to reveal to me what I need to surrender. He is faithful to do exactly that. The most difficult part of letting go for me is that I am not always ready to relinquish that particular "idol," but I know that I need to. I have only benefited in the end from surrendering EVERY area of my life. I have never had a time when I looked back and regretted giving God my all, and allowing Him to have full control. I know you will feel the same way as I have felt.

I encourage you to write down the areas that you are surrendering so that you may look back, months or years later, and thank God for what He did in your life. Use the space below to do exactly that; surrender fully!

"...but the humble in spirit will retain honor" (Proverbs 29:23).

"Draw near to God and He will draw near to you..." (James 4:8).

3. We didn't see God's name directly mentioned in these particular chapters, but we can surely see His hand at work. We can see it in the king's restless night. We can see it in how Mordecai was honored. Are there any other specific ways that you see God's hand directly at work?

4. Write a verse or verses that encouraged you this week.

5. Ask God to grow in you a character that reflects Who He is.

6. In looking back on the past week, is there a particular lesson that Lord has taught you? Was the lesson difficult to learn? Was it one that you learned from Haman's mistakes or Mordecai's example?

7. Another memory verse down! You are doing great! Keep memorizing the verses! Write down this week's verse.

"To the child of God, there is no such thing as accident. We travel an appointed way. When true faith enters, chance and mischance go out for good. The woman of true faith may live in the absolute assurance that her steps are ordered by the Lord." –A. W. Tozer[22]

Esther 7 and 8

"For I know the plans I have for you," says the Lord. *"They are plans for good and not for disaster, to give you a future and a hope. In those days when you pray, I will listen. If you look for me wholeheartedly, you will find me."*
(Jeremiah 29:11-13 NLT)

Day One

"...be sure your sin will find you out" (Numbers 32:23).

I like to say this verse as follows: "Beware, your sin will tell on you." We all can think of one time or another when this verse proved true in our own life. Indeed, our sin has a way of finding us out. Haman's sin did exactly that. Unfortunately for him, Haman's sin ended up costing him his life. We will even see that Haman's sin affected his family; his sons were executed because of Haman's actions. Sin will always affect others. We will see how true this is this week.

Make sure to go before the Lord in prayer before you start today's lesson.

1. Unfortunately, Haman is the first one to have his sins affect the lives of those around him and his immediate family. Fill in the table by reading the verses. Record the name of the person whose sin would have an effect on more than himself. Who was affected by this person's sin?

Verses	Main Person	People Affected
Genesis 3		
2 Samuel 11 2 Samuel 12:15-23		
2 Samuel 13		
Luke 15:11-32		

2. What problems could Esther have potentially faced since she had not been called before King Xerxes?

"She understands full well the delicate and precarious nature of her position. The threat against her and her people has two perpetrators, Haman and the king, and both are present with her. She must somehow fully expose the culpability of Haman, while at the same time never appearing in any way to be bringing any charges against the king. Hence, her response is extremely well thought out and presented with the utmost tact."[23]

When Esther approached the king a second time, knowing she couldn't put off her request any longer, I can only imagine what she was feeling. She had to have understood the weight of what she was about to ask. Esther humbly spoke to the king, becoming even more passionate as she explained the situation and her request.

"By long forbearance a ruler is persuaded, and a gentle tongue breaks a bone" (Proverbs 25:15).

Esther's patience, prayer and gentle words persuaded the king in her favor and the favor of her Jewish people. Elizabeth Elliot perfectly describes the actions that Esther displayed: "Restlessness and impatience change nothing except our peace and joy. Peace does not dwell in outward things, but in the heart prepared to wait trustfully and quietly on Him who has all things safely in His hands."[24]

Esther bluntly described Haman as *wicked*. I can see Haman's squirming in his seat as his fear grows greater and greater. He knew death was at hand for him.

3. Have you ever found yourself in a tough position like Esther? Did you answer the situation with prayer?

4. Haman allowed bitterness and resentment to get the better of him. He had been seeing himself as the second king. He had exalted himself in his own mind. Hebrews 12:15 describes what happens when we let bitterness take root in our life. Write Hebrews 12:15 in the space provided.

5. The Word of God describes the destiny of the wicked in many verses. What will happen to those who are evil? Write down a few lessons that you learned from each of the following verses.

Psalm 7:14-16

Psalm 9:17

Proverbs 10:27

Ecclesiastes 8:13

Isaiah 57:21

The greatest blessings will come when we are in the center of God's will. Once we are in His will, we are open to what He wants for us. Only then will we experience the real joy and peace that can only be found through Christ.

6. God has amazing plans for you and me! The promise of those plans is found in the memory verse for this week. Make sure to write down the verse!

Day Two

Today's lesson is one full of God's promises to His children. Personally, I love reading the promises that He made long ago with the forefathers of the Bible: Abraham, Isaac, Jacob, David and others! I am encouraged to hold fast to the promises that He has given me. If God fulfilled His Word to the forefathers, then why wouldn't He keep His promises to me?

What wonderful promises has He given to you? Are you trusting Him to fulfill ALL of His promises? If you are not trusting Him, then I encourage you to ask yourself "Why?"

Study His Word. Bask in the promises He has for you. Thank Him for the promises He has for you and the ones that He has fulfilled.

His Word is for you! Read the following verses and allow them to display His covenant with you!

> *"Therefore know that the LORD your God, He is God, the faithful God who keeps covenant and mercy for a thousand generations with those who love Him and keep His commandments"* (Deuteronomy 7:9).

> *"He who calls you is faithful, who also will do it"* (1 Thessalonians 5:24).

1. According to the following verses, what is God's view of the wicked?

    Psalm 5:4

    Psalm 7:11

    Proverbs 15:9

God had promised long ago that He would deliver the children of Israel. His promise for those who would harm the Israelites came true concerning the hanging of Haman.

Genesis 12:3, *"I will bless those who bless you, And I will curse him who curses you…."*

2. Haman's wickedness lines up with many of the verses in Proverbs. Pride and wickedness lead to its progressing, then being punished, and causing death in the final outcome. God does not let the wicked prosper forever; they will ultimately be punished. In Haman's case, his hatred and wicked heart led to his premature death. Each verse corresponds with a lesson to be learned from the verse. Match the verse with the proper statement.

_____ Proverbs 6:12-15   A) Wickedness being punished

_____ Proverbs 11:21   B) Wickedness causing death

_____ Proverbs 26:27   C) Wickedness progressing

_____ Psalm 1:6

_____ Proverbs 16:18

_____ Psalm 37:35, 36

_____ Ecclesiastes 8:13

"The LORD is King forever and ever; The nations have perished out of His land. [17]LORD, You have heard the desire of the humble; You will prepare their heart; You will cause Your ear to hear, [18]To do justice to the fatherless and the oppressed, the man of the earth may oppress no more" (Psalm 10:16-18).

3. Look up the word *wicked* in a dictionary, and write the definition in the space provided.

Wow! Quite the description, right?! I hope and pray that I will never see a day that my name will be associated with the word *wicked*. Unfortunately, Haman isn't the only person in the Bible to have an ugly character quality attached to his name.

4. What lessons can we learn from Haman?

5. How was Haman executed?

Haman's life demonstrates the truth of Galatians 6:7, which says, *"...for whatever a man sows, that he will also reap."* His judgment was served in the sentence of hanging, which is an extreme display of a death sentence.

"The nations have sunk down in the pit which they made; In the net which they hid, their own foot is caught. ^{16}The LORD is known by the judgment He executes; The wicked is snared in the work of his own hands" (Psalm 9:15, 16).

6. What ironic circumstances surrounded Haman's death?

"Behold, the wicked brings forth iniquity; Yes, he conceives trouble and brings forth falsehood. ^{15}He made a pit and dug it out, And has fallen into the ditch which he made. ^{16}His trouble shall return upon his own head, And his violent dealing shall come down on his own crown" (Psalm 7:14-16).

This promise came true in Esther's life. She saw firsthand what wickedness can do to a nation and how one person's wickedness can affect generations.

One of my favorite authors, Oswald Chambers, wisely wrote that "Everything the devil does, God overreaches to serve His own purpose."[25]

How true! God has much better plans that anything the Enemy could ever plan!

7. Psalm 37 describes the promises that God has in store for those who righteously follow Him. What are a few of the promises that you want to claim as your own or ones that speak to you?

8. How do Esther and Mordecai see justice begin to be put into place?

Day Three

Have you ever interceded before the Lord for yourself or on behalf of others? Esther is doing exactly that in chapter 8; she is going before the king on the behalf of her people. Even though Haman had been put to death, the edict that he devised and had decreed was still in motion.

Esther fell down before the king, and pleaded with him to save her people. Her husband listened to her heart, and he devised a way to help the Jews. I would tell you what happened, but I want you to find out for yourself during the next few days of study.

A new decree was the answer to the Jews' prayers. One woman named Esther changed the course of history through prayer, fasting, and boldness. God answered her prayer, but the nation of Israel would still have to go to battle against the other nations. We will not always get the answer we want; rather, He gives the answer that is the best for us. In Esther's case, she received her answer, but not quite in the way that she had hoped. However, you will see that He blessed their nation above and beyond what they could have ever dared to ask.

You may be asking the Lord for a specific answer to your prayer, and He didn't quite answer you in the way you had hoped. Let me remind you that His ways are nothing like your ways, and His thoughts are higher than your thoughts. He desires the best for your life. Thank Him today that He is answering the prayers in your life according to what He sees is best.

1. Esther could have asked the king for anything, but what did she request?

2. Notice how King Xerxes gave Haman his signet ring for Haman to do as he pleased. This decision of the king was not very wise. Solomon tells us that God will bring all things into judgment. Read Ecclesiastes 12:13, 14 and write the verses in the space provided.

3. Esther approached the king with grace and confidence. How can we approach our Heavenly Father Who cares for us more than Esther cared for her people? Read the following verses and write down the meaning of each Scripture.

   Hebrews 4:16

   Hebrews 10:19-22

4. Why couldn't the king reverse the decree that Haman had manipulated him to sign?

5. How did God provide for the Jewish people?

People have been trying to exterminate the Jews for centuries. The most commonly known attempt was the Holocaust. Adolf Hitler wanted nothing more than to entirely eradicate the entire Jewish community. I believe it is safe to consider Hitler a modern-day Haman. However, as in Esther's day, a man named Nicholas Winton stood against the Nazi regime during World War II and saved many Jewish children.

Nicholas was born in the early 1900s into a Jewish family living in London. During his older years, he traveled throughout Europe and even lived in Germany for a time. Once the threat of the Nazism began, he returned to Britain. When a friend told him of the Jewish children's desperate situation in Czechoslovakia, Nicholas Winton was able to save 669 children, most of them being Jewish. One brave man was able to save over 600 children.

Esther was given a similar circumstance—a choice to make—a God-ordained opportunity.

It's what you do with the opportunity that God has given you to make a difference that matters. Neither Esther nor Nicholas Winton turned away and ignored the grievous situation. They didn't say, "What will it matter? I am only one person." No, Esther and Nicholas Winton chose to take a stand. Their stand and courage saved hundreds and even thousands of lives.

6. What has God done in your life that you look back year after year and thank Him for doing?

7. God's timing is not the same as ours nor are His ways the same. Esther and Mordecai did not plan for things to turn out the way they did, but God did. His ways are the best! Write down Isaiah 55:8, 9 and commit these two verses to memory.

Day Four

Esther is a wonderful example of faithfulness to her family, her country, her people (the Jews), and her Lord. God certainly had prepared her for *"...such a time as this."* God has also prepared each one of us in advance. He knew exactly who you were before you were even born! He has a perfect plan for you each and every day. I challenge you to ask Him how you can faithfully serve Him each day starting with today. He wants to use you! He loves you!

1. How can you serve the Lord and be faithful to Him while you are waiting for Him to act?

2. Esther continues to show her dedication for the Jewish people despite the fact that her own life has been in danger time and time again. Esther trusted that God would be her strength and give her the courage she needed to save her people. Ask God to give you a courageous spirit to do what He has for you.

3. Write down Philippians 1:6.

"Then all peoples of the earth shall see that you are called by the name of the LORD, and they shall be afraid of you" (Deuteronomy 28:10).

4. God is secretly at work in this chapter—even while it may seem that everything is spinning out of control. Life is completely in His control. Nothing can happen unless He allows it. How can we see His control over everything in this chapter?

5. In what way did Mordecai's actions affect not only the Jews but also the Gentiles?

6. Esther shared her heart with the king and implored him on behalf of her people. What was the king's response? Do you feel that he really treasured his queen?

Isn't God amazing?! Each and every day, He will show you something new that He wants to show you. All you need to do is ask Him what He has for you to learn today. I encourage you to do exactly that! Ask Him to show you what He has in store for you today and write down precisely what He says.

Day Five

Prayer is an important discipline in the life of every believer. Prayer is one way that we can talk to God, but it also allows us to be a part of God's work in our life firsthand. Prayer is a way that we can lift up others to Him, express our joys and trials, and ask for His help.

Prayer is such a wonderful discipline! Esther and Mordecai knew the only way they could save their people was through God's help.

How often do you go before the Lord in prayer? Is your praying only for yourself or for others too? Have you noticed situations changing? Did you notice that you changed how you feel about others?

When I have a particular trial in my life and I go before the Lord in prayer, I notice that I am the one who needs the most changing. Yes, others may need it too, but the changing has to start with you. Esther's change started with her; she took that first step though prayer, and the Lord used her in such a mighty, amazing way!

1. Read the following verses and write down a short summary of what you have learned and wish to apply to your life from each verse. A great idea to consider is writing down how you can directly and currently apply a few of these verses to your life.

   Philippians 4:6, 7

   Isaiah 40:29-31

Romans 12:12

Psalm 18:6

Psalm 145:18

2. I want you to write a prayer asking the Lord to make you a mighty prayer warrior for Him!

3. How did the Lord show the Jewish nation His faithfulness in Esther chapters 7 and 8?

4. Read 2 Corinthians 4:7-9 and describe how these verses perfectly apply to Israel's predicament.

5. What are a few ways that you can display God's faithfulness in your life in spite of the current circumstances in your life?

6. What do these quotes by Andrew Murray mean to you?

"Let every approach to God, and every request for fellowship with Him be accompanied by a new, very definite, and entire surrender to Him to work in you." [26]

"Beware in your prayers, above everything else, of limiting God, not only by unbelief, but by fancying that you know what He can do. Expect unexpected things 'above all that we ask or think.' " [27]

7. Write down this week's memory verse from memory.

Can you believe that we only have one more week of study?! I pray that you have been using this study to its fullest advantage and allowing God to show you something new each day. I know that it is not easy to complete each day's task as daily duties and responsibilities tend to get in the way, but great job for pressing through it all!

Most times when I try to work on my Bible study, I find many seemingly pressing matters will easily take me away from my lesson. I encourage you that when it happens to try your best to complete that task later if possible or make sure that you come back and finish the study. When I give 110 percent to my Bible studies is when I find I learn the most about Who God is, and what He is trying to teach me. My encouragement to you this week is to keep pressing on in your study!

Esther 9 and 10

"What shall we say about such wonderful things as these?
If God is for us, who can ever be against us?"

(Romans 8:31 NLT)

Day One

Today's lesson is based on another of my favorite verses: Matthew 19:26, *"But Jesus looked at them and said to them, 'With men this is impossible, but with God all things are possible.' "*

The Jews are at the brink of death. Their lives were placed into the hands of their enemies by Haman's wicked plot. The situation looked hopeless for the Jewish people. However, what looked impossible for His children was not impossible for Him.

Read and highlight Matthew 19:26. Allow the Lord to show you that with Him *all* things are possible. Before you start your lesson today, I want you to pray Matthew 19:26 for your life, and ask the Lord to bring this verse alive in your life.

1. How did the king combat the edict that Haman had put in place?

2. Why could no one beat the Jews?

3. Write down Romans 8:31.

God had His hand over the whole decree and the battle. He knew the outcome was in His perfect plan. Romans 8:31 says, *"...If God is for us, then who can be against us?"* and the Jews knew their God would protect them—as He had promised Joshua in Joshua 10:8, which says, *"And the LORD said to Joshua, 'Do not fear them, for I have delivered them into your hand; not a man of them shall stand before you.' "*

4. Write down how knowing that God is on our side and will protect us encourages you.

5. Haman did what was evil in the sight of the Lord. The Bible says that the sins of the parents will affect their children. Read Exodus 20:5 and write the verse in the space provided.

6. The Jews fought the battle, but the Lord gave the victory! According to chapter 9, how many men did the Jews kill?

7. What is the importance of Purim?

Purim is celebrated each year during the Hebrew month of Adar (late winter/early spring) on the fourteenth day. Usually Purim falls in March. The festival of Purim celebrates the time when Mordecai saved the Jews from Haman's plot to destroy all of the Jews.

During Purim, the Jewish people read the book of Esther on the eve of Purim and the morning of Purim, gifts are given to the poor, good gifts are given to their friends, and a

Purim feast is held. The Fast of Esther precedes the celebration of Purim—from sunrise to sunset just as it did in the book of Esther.

> "Now it was God's intent that a last conflict should take place between Israel and Amalek the conflict which began with Joshua in the desert was to be finished by Mordecai in the king's palace." – Charles Spurgeon[28]

8. Romans 8:31 is one of my favorite verses! If God is for me, then who can ever be against me?

   I encourage you to write down this verse a few times to help you better remember its truth.

Day Two

What is your life verse? I define a life verse as one that remains very meaningful to you through all of the different experiences in your life. This verse is an encouragement to you through the great times and through the bad times. My life verse is Romans 8:28, which says, *"And we know that all things work together for good to those who love God, to those who are the called according to his purpose."* This verse has proven true many times in my life! Knowing that God is working everything for my good despite what the circumstances depict in front of me encourages me greatly! Simply recognize and know that everything is working together for your good, and whatever comes into your life is growing you more toward Christ and the woman that He desires you to become.

If you don't have a life verse yet, then I encourage you to pray about which one you would have to be your verse. Ask the Lord to specifically show you which one He would have for you!

If you do have a life verse, then make sure to commit it to memory! That way when the trials of life come, you are ready to combat them with the Word of God!

Prayer is the most important aspect of each day! It's our way of communicating with our Savior! Don't forget to start with prayer before today's lesson gets underway!

1. How did God use Esther in His timing and purpose?

2. What did the book of Esther teach you about the Lord?

3. What qualities did you see in Esther throughout the book?

4. Write a note to God, thanking Him for all of the blessings He has given to you.

Psalm 30:5, *"...Weeping may endure for a night, But joy comes in the morning."*

5. God showed His faithfulness in Esther's life, and He will do the same for each of us. Write down Hebrews 10:23 as a promise that He will always be faithful even when we are faithless.

6. How has God proved Himself faithful to you in your life?

What does it mean to be *faithful*? Do you know anyone who has been a great example to you in this area? Well, to start, take a look at the following definitions from Dictionary.com:

Faithful:

- "True to one's word, promises, vows, etc."
- "Steady in allegiance or affection; loyal; constant"
- "Reliable, trusted, or believed"

All of these descriptions perfectly fit the attributes of God! He is faithful! He is true to His Word. He keeps His promises. He is faithful even when we are faithless. He is reliable. He is trustworthy. He is loyal. He is constant. He will never ever fail us. Aren't these qualities of God so encouraging?!

7. As you read through the book of Esther, you should have noticed that you did not see any direct references to God's name—not even once. However, God's hand can surely be seen through Esther, Mordecai, and the Jewish people. Write down a few ways that you saw His hand displayed in their lives.

Day Three

Hebrews 11 is known as the "Hall of Faith" chapter. If you look at the countless examples of names, you will see they were clearly far from being perfect. However, perfection did not put them in the Hall of Faith; rather, each person's faith in the Lord Jesus Christ placed them in this chapter.

How is your faith doing? Does it need some improvement? I know I can always use more faith in every area of my life. Ask God to instill in you a spirit of faith—one that doesn't fail when the storms come, and one that clings tightly to Him.

"Now faith is confidence in what we hope for and assurance about what we do not see" (Hebrews 11:1 NIV).

1. Esther displayed an incredible amount of faith throughout the book named for her. God blessed Esther tremendously because of her faith. Read Hebrews 11 in your Bible. Circle the word *faith* every time you come across it. How many times is the word used in chapter 11?

2. Why is having faith in God so important?

3. How can we have the same faith in God that Esther possessed?

God shows in the book of Esther how He can take people of seemingly little importance and use them mightily. Esther and Mordecai are great examples of this principle. He uses those who are nothing, so that, with Him, we will be something. If we determine that we are great, there will be no room for God to show others how awesome and powerful He is. However, when we become like the least of these, then God can truly use us.

4. How does God use ordinary people for His extraordinary work? Think of a few examples found in the Bible and briefly write down about how the Lord used each person.

5. What did the book of Esther teach you about how God works in mysterious ways and through ordinary people?

"It has been well said that the book of Esther is a record of wonders without a miracle, and therefore, though equally revealing the glory of the Lord, it sets forth in another fashion from that which is displayed in the overthrow of Pharaoh by miraculous power." – Charles Spurgeon[29]

6. Our God is amazing, isn't He?!! He uses the foolish things of this world to confound the wise. Read the following verses and fill in the blanks.

"The Lord will cause your _____ who rise against you to be _____ before your face; they shall come out against you one way and flee before you _____ _____. [10]Then all peoples of the earth shall see that you are _____ by the name of the _____, and they shall be afraid of you. [11]And the _____ will grant you plenty of goods, in the fruit of your body, in the increase of your _____ , and in the produce of your ground, in the land of which the Lord swore to your _____ to give you" (Deuteronomy 28:7, 10-11).

"But God has chosen the _____ _____ of the _____ to put to shame the _____, and _____ has chosen the weak things of the world to put to _____ the things which are _____" (1 Corinthians 1:27).

"Listen, my dear brothers and sisters: Has not _____ _____ those who are poor in the eyes of the _____ to be rich in _____ and to inherit the _____ he _____ those who love him?" (James 2:5 NIV).

7. Using the timeline on the next page, write down the order of events which occurred in the book of Esther.

Esther Timeline

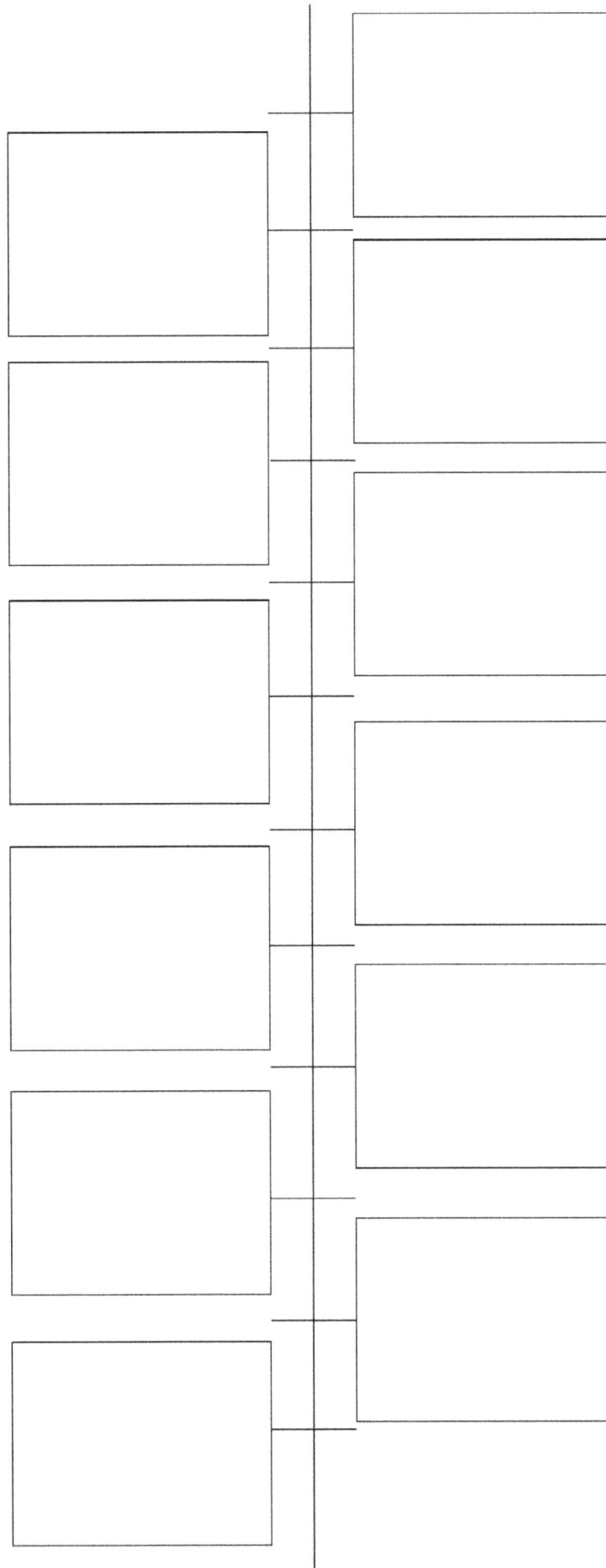

Day Four

"And we know that all things work together for good to those who love God, to those who are the called according to His purpose" (Romans 8:28).

God worked everything for the good in Esther's life. We see how the story begins and ends, but Esther lived it! She saw God working firsthand in her life. Esther allowed God to use her in whatever capacity He would choose for her. God used unlikely people and makes them great. He uses the foolish things of the world to confound the wise. God really does use everything for our good.

1. How did Esther use her position as queen to influence King Xerxes for good?

2. We all have the ability to influence those around us. How can you use your influence for good like Esther did with the king and Mordecai did with Esther?

The Lord has given each one of us the ability to use our influence for good or for bad. Esther used her queenship as a way to help her people.

I particularly admire one wife mentioned in the Bible for using her influence to save her husband's life. I Samuel 25 describes Abigail as an intelligent and beautiful woman; however, the description for her husband Nabal is quite the opposite; he is described as being surly and mean, especially in his dealings with others.

You can read the full story in 1 Samuel 25 for yourself, but I will briefly paraphrase what is happening with three principal characters: David, Abigail, and Nabal. David and his men had been out in the wilderness, and they came upon Nabal's land. David sent ten of his men to find favor with Nabal. However, Nabal refused them food and drink. David became furious that Nabal would insult him with his refusal. Word reached Abigail, Nabal's wife, of her husband's refusal, and she quickly gathered food and took it to David and his men. Her quick and thoughtful gesture saved not only her husband's life but her own.

Abigail's ability to use her influence for good is a wonderful example for us. We can use our influence at work, school, and in our marriage for good.

Ask the Lord to help you become a woman of influence in the lives of others.

3. From what example did Esther display that you learned the most?

Esther's continuous faith and trust in God were the greatest example in my life. She trusted God when her life was at stake. She had faith that God was working in her life.

Trusting the Lord has been an area in my life on which I have been working because trusting Him doesn't always come easy for me. I asked the Lord to instill in me that trust and faith that Esther displayed, and He did just that! He wants to grow you in His image. Ask the Lord to help you be the example to others like you previously wrote.

4. We can see Proverbs 21:1 perfectly illustrated in the book of Esther. In what ways did you this happening throughout the entire book?

5. Read Psalm 37. Write down the promises that God has for those who are faithful to Him.

6. Delve a little deeper into Psalm 37 and write down what God tell us about the wicked.

7. How do Mordecai's and Esther's lives challenge you to take the steps of faith in the direction that God calls you?

Day Five

The entire book of Esther has taught me some important lessons. Perhaps the most important lesson is the faithfulness of God and His work in our life.

Esther prayed through her problems, faced her fears, and ultimately saved the nation of Israel with the Lord's help. Time and time again, His hand is all over this book.

"Continue earnestly in prayer, being vigilant in it with thanksgiving" (Colossians 4:2).

1. After reading the following passage, describe the joy that comes with serving the Lord.

   "Oh, clap your hands, all you peoples! Shout to God with the voice of triumph! [2]For the LORD Most High is awesome; He is a great King over all the earth. [3]He will subdue the peoples under us, and the nations under our feet. [4]He will choose our inheritance for us, the excellence of Jacob whom He loves. Selah

   [5]God has gone up with a shout, the LORD with the sound of a trumpet. [6]Sing praises to God, sing praises! Sing praises to our King, sing praises! [7]For God is the King of all the earth; Sing praises with understanding.

   [8]God reigns over the nations; God sits on His holy throne. [9]The princes of the people have gathered together. The people of the God of Abraham. For the shields of the earth belong to God; He is greatly exalted" (Psalm 47).

2. Write down the definition of *vindicate*. What does the word have to do with the Jews winning the battle in Esther chapter 9?

3. How did the Lord abundantly provide for the Jews at the end of Esther chapters 9 and 10?

The Lord more than abundantly provides for His children! Job and Joseph, my favorite Old Testament examples, show the Lord's blessing on His children. Job lost everything—his land, his children, his wife, his livestock, his health and his friends—through a trial the Lord allowed him to experience. Still, Job still trusted the Lord, and the Lord blessed him and restored to him twice as much as he once had.

When Joseph's brothers sold him into slavery, he lost his family and his freedom. At the end of Joseph's story, though, we see God placed him in second-in-command over all of Egypt, blessed him with a wife and children, and restored his relationships with his father and brothers.

God has poured His blessings on your life as well! Take a few minutes and think about all of the wonderful ways Lord has blessed you, and thank Him for blessing you. Then, write down these blessings, and later you will be able to look back and see exactly how He showered your life with many good things!

4. Think about all you have learned throughout this Bible study. Write down one or two truths that you felt the Lord really impressed on you about who YOU are, what you need to change, and a character discipline you have begun to instill or even a verse that ministered to you.

5. The Lord used Ruth and Esther to shine a light for Him in their generation! How can you be a light to those around you? How can you display to others the love that Christ has shown you?

You did it! You completed the study, and you memorized His Word along the way. I hope you remember the verses because I want you to write down each verse you memorized from memory in the space provided.

   1. Ruth 1:16

   2. Proverbs 31:30, 31

   3. Numbers 6:24-26

4. Psalm 34:19

5. 1 Samuel 2:30b

6. Jeremiah 29:11-13

7. Romans 8:31

I am so proud of you for finishing strong!! You did it!! You completed a study that I hope has shown you quite a few truths. Four of the truths that have become more real to me are as follows:

- His faithfulness in every situation
- His love, protection, and provision
- He is the only One Who can instill insights into our life.
- He works all things for our good.

(Feel free to add the truths you have learned to this list as well.)

Endnotes

[1]A. W. Tozer, *Man, the Dwelling Place of God* (Harrisburg, Penn.: Christian Publications, 1966), n.p.

[2]Frances Vander Velde, *Women of the Bible* (Grand Rapids: Kregel, 1985), 104.

[3]"Christian Classics Ethereal Library," 2005, http://www.ccel.org/ccel/spurgeon/sermons46 .xxv.html,

[4]Larry Crabb, *Shattered Dreams: God's Unexpected Path to Joy* (Colorado Springs: WaterBrook, 2011), 68.

[5]Elizabeth George, *Women Who Loved God: A Devotional Walk with the Women of the Bible* (Eugene, Ore.: Harvest House Publishers, 1999), May 21

[6]Warren W. Wiersbe, *Be Committed: Doing God's Will Whatever the Cost* (Colorado Springs: David C. Cook, 2008), 27.

[7]Adam Clark, *Clark's Commentary*, 1831, http://biblehub.com/commentaries/clarke/ruth/3.htm, accessed 7 July 2015.

[8]Leon Morris, "Ruth 3: Ruth and Boaz at the Threshing Floor, 1-18" *Walking With Giants*, 2015, http://www.walkingwithgiants.net/bible-study-notes/old-testament/ruth/ruth-3/, accessed 7 July 2015.

[9]John MacArthur, *The MacArthur Bible Commentary* (Nashville: Thomas Nelson, Inc., 2005), 730.

[10]Marvin Breneman, *The New American Commentary: Ezra, Nehemiah, Esther.* Vol. 10. Ed. E. Ray Clendenen (Nashville: B&H Publishing Group, 1993), 314.

[11]Pamela Rose Williams, "Corrie ten Boom: 24 Quotes," 2013. http://www.what christianswanttoknow.com/corrie-ten-boom-quotes-24-favorites, accessed 14 July 2015.

[12]Matt Chandler, Josh Patterson, and Eric Geiger. *Creature of the Word: The Jesus-Centered Church* (Nashville: B&H Publishing Group, 2012), 176.

[13]Mark Batterson, *In a Pit with a Lion on a Snowy Day: How to Survive and Thrive When Opportunity Roars* (Sisters, Ore.: Multnomah Books, 2006), 32.

[14]Arthur T. Pierson, *George Müller of Bristol: And His Witness to a Prayer-hearing God* (New York: Baker & Taylor, 1899), 293.

[15]One estimate is that Müller collected about $150 million in today's currency. Thanks to Coty Pinckney for the reference and calculations, using John J. McCusker's, "Comparing the Purchasing Power of Money in Great Britain from 1264 to Any Other Year Including the Present," *Economic History Services, 2001;* "George Mueller's Strategy for Showing God Simplicity of Faith, Sacred Scripture, and Satisfaction in God," 3 February 2014, http://www.desiringgod.org/biographies/george-muellers-strategy-for-showing-god#28, accessed 14 July 2015.

[16]Charles H. Spurgeon, *Sermons on Women of the Bible* (Peabody, Mass.: Hendrickson Publishers, Inc., 2008), 154.

[17]Raelyn Tan, "18 Franklin D Roosevelt Quotes to Inspire You," http://burningforsuccess. com/franklin-d-roosevelt-quotes/, accessed 14 July 2015.

[18]Spurgeon, *Sermons on Women of the Bible*, 154.

[19]Adam Clarke, *The Holy Bible: Containing the Old and New Testaments: The Text Printed from the Most Correct Copies of the Present Authorized Translation including the Marginal and Parallel Texts; with a Commentary and Critical Notes Designed as a Help to a Better Understanding of the Sacred Writings* (New York: J. Emory and B. Waugh for the Methodist Episcopal Church, 1831), 819.

[20]Andrew Murray, *Waiting on God* (Springdale, Penn.: Whitaker House, 1983), 62.

[21]Adam Clarke, *Commentary on the Bible*, 1831, http://www.sacredtexts.com/bib/cmt/clarke/est002.htm , accessed 15 July 2015.

[22]A. W. Tozer, *We Travel an Appointed Way: Making Spiritual Progress* (Camp Hill, Penn.: Christian Publications, 1988), 7.

[23]Frederic W. Bush, *Word Biblical Commentary*, Vol. 9 (Nashville: Thomas Nelson Publishers, 1996), 431.

[24]Debbie McDaniel, "40 Inspiring Quotes from Elisabeth Elliot, 2015, http://www. crosswalk.com/faith/spiritual-life/40-inspiring-quotes-from-elisabeth-elliot.html, accessed 15 July 2015.

[25]Leah Case, "The Chosen Life: Studies in Esther, 2005, http://www.harvest.org/pdf/studies-in-esther12/lesson-7/225.pdf, accessed 15, July 2015.

[26]Murray, Andrew. "Daily Fellowship with God." *Andrew Murray on the Holy Spirt*. New Kensington: Whitaker House, 1998. N. pag. Print.

[27]"Everyday Myths of Prayer." *When I Pray, What Does God Do?* N.p.: Monarch, 2015. 45. Print.

[28]Charles H. Spurgeon, *The Metropolitan Tabernacle Pulpit: Sermons* (London: Passmore & Alabaster, 1856), 614.

[29]Spurgeon, *Sermons on Women of the Bible*, 151.

Naomi's Family Tree

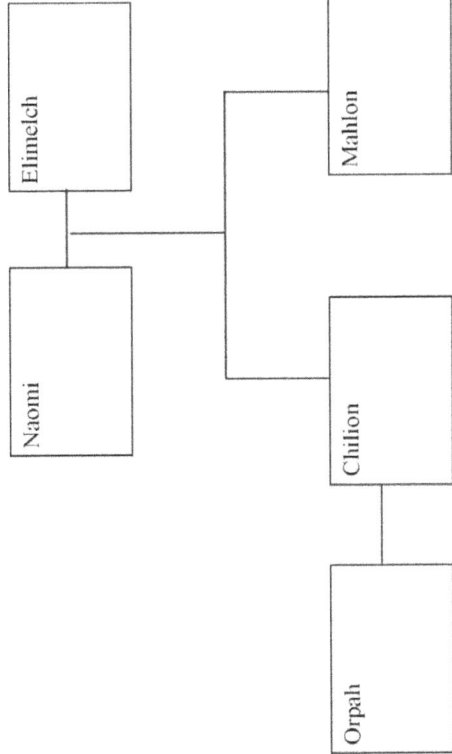

Boaz's Family Tree

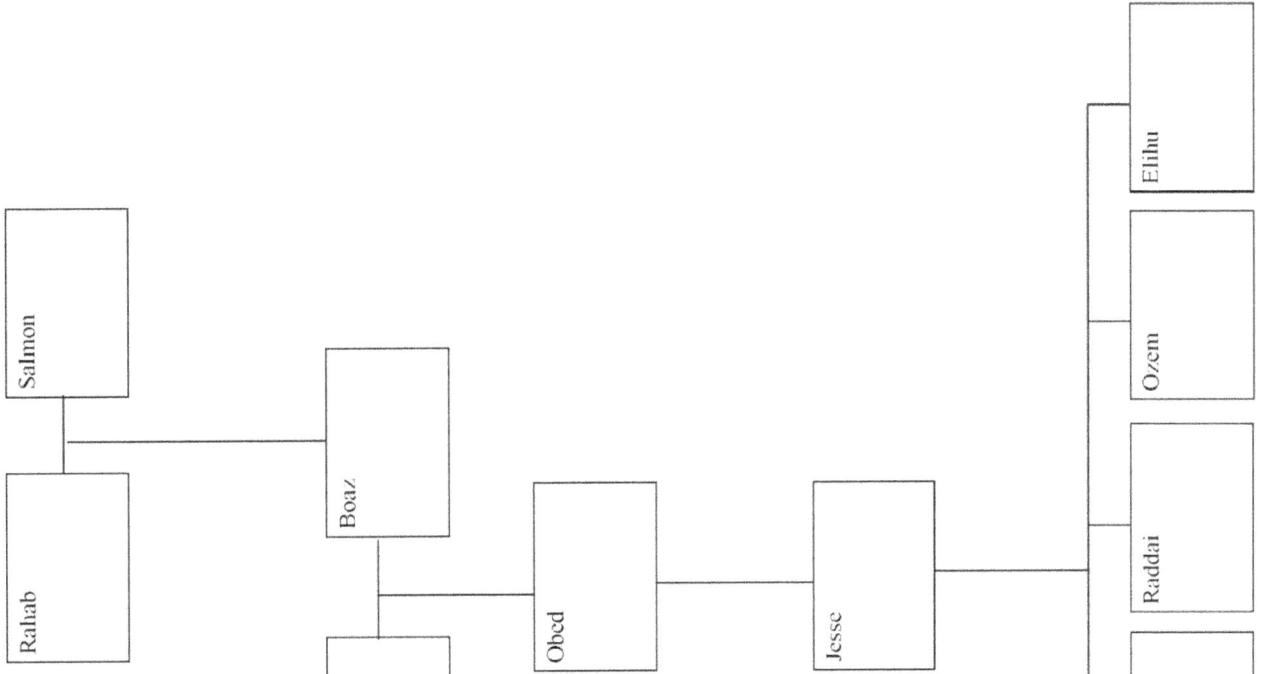

```
Naomi — Elimelech                          Rahab — Salmon

        |                                         |
   Orpah — Chilion    Mahlon — Ruth  ─────────  Boaz
                                  |
                                Obed
                                  |
                                Jesse
                                  |
  ┌────┬────────┬──────┬───────┬───────┬──────┬──────┬───────┐
David  Abinadab  Eliab  Shimea  Nethanel  Raddai  Ozem  Elihu
```

Esther's Timeline

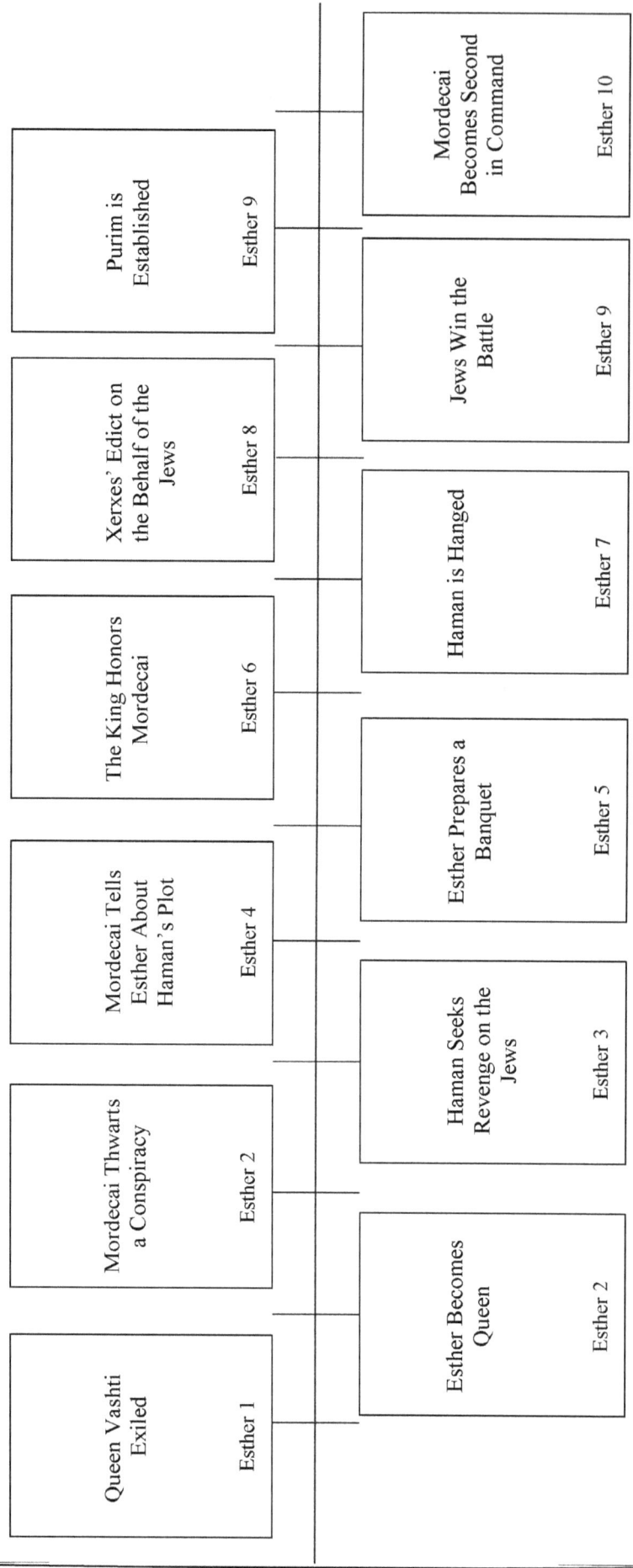

Queen Vashti Exiled	Mordecai Thwarts a Conspiracy	Mordecai Tells Esther About Haman's Plot	The King Honors Mordecai	Xerxes' Edict on the Behalf of the Jews	Purim is Established
Esther 1	Esther 2	Esther 4	Esther 6	Esther 8	Esther 9

Esther Becomes Queen	Haman Seeks Revenge on the Jews	Esther Prepares a Banquet	Haman is Hanged	Jews Win the Battle	Mordecai Becomes Second in Command
Esther 2	Esther 3	Esther 5	Esther 7	Esther 9	Esther 10

Connect with Caitlyn

Read more at my website:

valuedandesteemd.com

If you have been encouraged by the Bible study, have questions, need prayer, or have any comments, I would love to hear from you! I will respond to each email as soon as possible! I can't wait to hear from you!

valuedandesteemed@gmail.com

Follow Me on Social Media

Instagram: valued_and_esteemed

Facebook: Valued and Esteemed

Twitter: Caitlyn_Burns_

Youtube: Caitlyn Burns

www.ingramcontent.com/pod-product-compliance
Lightning Source LLC
Chambersburg PA
CBHW081151090426
42736CB00017B/3271